# LIVING WATERS
## The Springs of Missouri

# LIVING WATERS
## The Springs of Missouri

BY

## LORING BULLARD

Foreword by
Mike Kromrey, Executive Director
Watershed Committee
of the Ozarks

The Ozarks Studies Institute of
Missouri State University
Springfield, Missouri
2020

**Published by the Ozarks Studies Institute,** an initiative of the Missouri State University Libraries.
© 2020 Missouri State University. For inquiries, contact:
    Duane G. Meyer Library
    901 South National Library
    Springfield, MO 65897
    417.836.4525

Book cover and layout design by Jeanne Simpson

ISBN-13: 978-1-7346290-0-2

Library of Congress Cataloging-in-Publication Data:
Names: Bullard, Loring, author.
Title: Living waters : the springs of Missouri / by Loring Bullard.
Description: Springfield, Missouri : Ozarks Studies Institute, 2020. | Includes bibliographical references.
Identifiers: ISBN 978-1-7346290-0-2
Subjects: LCSH: Springs—Missouri.
Classification: LCC GB1198.3.M8 B85 2020 | DDC 551.49809778—dc23

The OSI Publications Series in Ozarks History and Culture, Volume 3.

The Ozarks Studies Institute (OSI) of Missouri State University seeks to preserve the heritage of the Ozarks, its culture, environment, and history by fostering a comprehensive knowledge of Ozarks' peoples, places, characteristics, and dynamics. The Institute promotes a sense of place for residents and visitors alike and serves as an educational resource by collecting existing—and discovering new—knowledge about the Ozarks and by providing access to that knowledge. *Living Waters* is third in the OSI series.

Forthcoming from the OSI:
*"We Gave Them Thunder": Marmaduke's Raid and the Civil War in Missouri and Arkansas,* by William Garrett Piston and John C. Rutherford.

The Ozarks Studies Institute is proud to partner with the Watershed Committee of the Ozarks in celebrating, teaching about, and working to protect Missouri's streams. For further information, contact:
    Watershed Committee of the Ozarks
    2400 East Valley Water Mill Road
    Springfield, MO 65803

*In memory of*
Jerry D. Vineyard
*and*
Oscar "Oz" Hawksley

## FOREWORD

I BET YOU'VE FELT THE PULL OF WATER—the urge to linger by the lake a little longer; or you've felt it drifting down a river in your canoe, or just sitting by the water. The effect water has on us is deep, and hard to fully articulate or even grasp. Water is so integral to our survival as a species that I suspect the way we perceive and feel about it is as much a product of deep-seated instincts and genetic knowledge as it is rational thought. As seen on a map, the dense gathering of our human family across parts of the globe reflects the nearly gravitational pull of water on a massive scale. It has been that way since the beginning.

On a recent hike to a spring in the Ozark Hills, I gazed into the clear, cool water. The polished gravel on the bottom of the spring branch danced in the water's sight-bending motion. The words of Thomas McGuane came to mind: "every refractive slide of cold water a glimpse of eternity." One particular rock caught my eye. I reached into the water and clutched the whitish piece of chert-stone. My heart fluttered as I realized that this tapered, fluted, one-in-a-million rock had actually been crafted by human hands. It was a projectile point, and a tactile reminder of what we already know—springs have attracted people since the dawn of human existence.

My home, the city of Springfield (or Spring-Field, as I think of it), owes its very existence to the cool waters which flow from beneath. As the story goes, Native Americans showed a newcomer, John Polk Campbell, the spring-filled valley of Jordan Creek. The land and water so inspired Campbell that he carved his initials on an ash tree to claim the property, his future homestead, where he would move his family and which would eventually grow into the Queen City of the Ozarks. Central to this homestead was what we would today call a karst window, a rocky skylight, opening downward into the plumbing system of a spring, a "natural well of wonderful depth."

Later, the waters of Jordan Creek were tarnished with sewage and stormwater, and recurring floods destroyed buildings and property in its floodplain. Through an early version of hydrologic problem solving, citizens embarked on a major public works project to "conduct the waters peaceably underground," which is where Jordan Creek and the natural well remain today. However, the revival of Jordan Creek is now underway. It is being exhumed from its concrete catacombs. Its waters are once again finding sunlight, and a part of our community's heritage is being returned to us. This "daylighting" is an investment in Springfield's more promising future, and an acknowledgment that citizens support the rejuvenation of our founding waters, including the city's sparkling springs.

*Bull Creek. Photo by Kyle Kosovich.*

Technology, coupled with a deeply rooted desire to explore caves and springs, continues the story in ways that John Polk Campbell or Native Americans surely never imagined. The Ozark Cave Diving Alliance, a small but dedicated band of explorers, now presses the limits of exploration by heading down into the depths of springs using SCUBA gear, extra oxygen, high tech equipment and, thankfully, cameras. I'll never forget the picture taken by one of their divers from below the surface of Bennett Spring—the most beautiful blue color framed by the blackness of the cave; the silhouettes of many trout, as if floating in a blue hole of space.

While we are often human-centric in our thoughts and musings about springs, they are very important for non-human life, particularly fish. Take for example the blind cave fish. This organism has adapted through the eons to inhabit the springs, caves, and aquifers beneath our feet. Bass and "googleye" seek springs out in the winter, because water from springs stays relatively warm. To learn more about this phenomenon, researchers used radio telemetry on the Current and Jacks Fork Rivers to see just how far smallmouth bass would travel to reach the springs they inhabit to ride out the winter. The results were astonishing. Some of the transmitter-equipped bass traveled over 50 miles from where they were tagged at their winter refuge in Big Spring to their summer hang-outs. Many of those fish then returned to Big Spring the following fall to ride out the winter, including one fish that made a 70-mile journey from the Jacks Fork in just one week. Another fish, on its third (recorded) human encounter, ended up in an angler's freezer. These data points illustrate that springs are at the center of the smallmouth's orbit.

For Loring Bullard, water has been a common thread throughout his life. At Central Missouri State College (now University of Central Missouri), he was a student of the great teacher and biologist, Oz Hawksley. Oz was a dedicated river runner and lifelong advocate for Missouri streams. His expeditions were always a combination of exploration, adventure, and research. In fact, he published the first paddler's guide to Missouri's Ozark streams. Oz was a long-time friend and mentor to Loring, and his work continues to benefit those who dip paddles into Missouri streams.

For Loring, trips with Oz were starting points for a lifetime of river exploration. Loring has paddled many of our nation's great rivers, including the Colorado, Yampa, Gauley, Salmon and Snake, and other rivers from Alaska to West Virginia to the desert canyon of the Salt River in Arizona. These experiences and the perspectives gained by them on rivers, watersheds, and landscapes, both physical and cultural, constitute a lifelong journey of learning.

Loring became Executive Director of the Watershed Committee of the Ozarks in 1989. He accomplished a great deal during his professional career and the way he did it was, well, river-like. As he continued along, he gathered partners, consensus, and momentum for the cause, and like flowing water, slowly eroded difficult barriers. One of his crowning achievements was the Watershed Center at Valley Water Mill Park, which continues to grow and pay dividends today.

The Watershed Center truly is a microcosm of the Ozarks. Each year, thousands of students and visitors experience springs, nature, and a native Ozark landscape there. Loring understood that stewardship of water and the earth is a tall order unless there is a firm connection in people's hearts and minds to the resources we want them to care for and protect. In recognition of this need, education programs at the Watershed Center are place-based, interactive, and experiential, with water as a unifying theme. Each program is tailored to compliment the needs of the students and educators. With the increasing number and effectiveness of programs, hundreds more seeds of stewardship are planted and fertilized every year.

Loring recognized that Sanders Spring, at the heart of the Watershed Center, could be an oasis of interactive potential, so it became one of the site's first "learning stations." Springs have been at the center of Loring's passion ever since. For this book, he avidly searched out springs all over the state, learned their histories, and developed new friendships with people who shared his fascination with them. What you will experience in the following pages is, in my opinion, a masterpiece—a rare confluence of experience, passion, and skillful writing. It tells the story of humanity's ever flowing, ever changing journey with springs. Human interactions with springs over time are often just as intriguing as the springs themselves. Those stories, along with beautiful photos and careful explanations of how springs form and function, will help readers enjoy these remarkable "living waters" in a deeper way. Reading this book, in fact, is like sitting in a canoe with Loring. The flow is easy, and the fascinating stories never end.

*Mike Kromrey*
*Executive Director*
*Watershed Committee*
*of the Ozarks*

# TABLE OF CONTENTS

*Alley Spring. Photo by Gayle Harper.*

*Pioneer Spring. Photo by Steve Spencer.*

# PROLOGUE

A MAN STOOD ALONE ON A DRY RIDGE. His feet were covered in dust. His furry vest hung in tatters from his shoulders. Blood oozed from wounds on his bare ankles and chest, and dried blood caked his upper arm, which ached and throbbed. His lips were cracked and bleeding, his tongue so swollen that he could barely breathe. Through bloodshot eyes, he strained to see the southern horizon, where he hoped to see smoke rising—but none appeared. At this point, he wasn't sure he could make it home.

He wasn't even sure he had a home—or at least that anyone would be there when he arrived. Many days ago, before he had left with his brother to hunt, there had been talk in the group of moving. The rocky shelter where they lived provided deep shade and breezes in hot weather and with a fire banked in front, precious warmth in winter. But the surrounding lands were changing—they could all see it, sense it. The dryness had been creeping back over the last several seasons—more dead and dying trees on the ridges, hardly any flow in the creeks, grasses brown and crackling. Game had diminished significantly, and the men had to travel farther and farther to hunt for food.

That's where the man and his brother had been. They had tracked a bull elk for two days, finally cornering it at the one place they knew it would have to return to, sooner or later—the waterhole; really just a seep, a murky puddle overflowing a rocky pocket. They were able to perch themselves above the seep, downwind, and at the critical time, with a pre-arranged signal, the man's brother delivered the piercing blow, deeply wounding the big animal. It lunged, and bawled, and staggered and crashed through small trees before stopping, standing unsteadily, wheezing, blood gushing from the jagged gash in its side.

Without hesitation, the man had run toward the elk, thrusting his spear into its swollen neck. But the big brute had fight left in him, and wheeled and charged and with his sprawling rack had rammed and then pitched the man like a rag doll. His brother had then lunged in with his spear, but the elk wasn't done. He reared and kicked the brother's chest, knocking him to the ground, then lowered his head and impaled the brother on the rigid tines of his antlers. With that, the beast let out a long rattling sigh before crumpling to the ground, heaving its last dying gasps.

The man dragged the elk off of his dead brother. He then knelt and touched his brother's eyes and squeezed his hand. From the leather pouch on his brother's belt, he carefully removed the polished, sharply fluted stone and put it into his own pouch. He knelt over the elk and cut off some

*An Inca Spring. Photo by Loring Bullard.*

of the meat, wrapping it in a skin that he could sling over his shoulder. He turned away, examined his own wounds, and then limped over to take a long drink from the stagnant pool. After several minutes, resting in the sparse shade, chest heaving, he turned to the south, toward home.

*Points. Courtesy of Jack Ray, Center for Archaeological Research, Missouri State University.*

His wounds were severe, and in the heat he quickly became dehydrated. He began to stagger, wondering whether he would survive the journey. There was no water anywhere to quench his thirst. He licked the dew, if he saw any, from grasses and leaves. The creeks were bone dry, and even digging among the chert cobbles in the stream bed yielded no moisture. Finally, after two days of struggling in the desert-like heat, he came upon the ridge—the last hill before home.

But what would he find there? The group, including the man and his brother, had already made a plan before they left. If the spring—their only remaining water source—dried up any more, they would be forced to leave. The man feared that the group had already decided that he and his brother weren't coming home—that they had packed up their few essentials and left, searching for the closest group of kin, who they hoped were still living many miles to the north, or east. But without water, the man doubted he would have enough time left to find them.

He climbed up on a low limestone ledge atop the ridge, using stunted, twisted oak trees as handholds. He arched his aching back, rubbed his eyes and looked again, and then, miraculously, saw a slender wisp of smoke rising above the trees in the distance, right where he knew his family should be. In spite of his wounds and powerful thirst, a modicum of hope began to rise within him.

He staggered toward home. A half-mile or so before he got there, he skirted by the spring. Thankfully, it still flowed, although very feebly. A thin green ribbon of slender reeds lined the murky branch where it meandered toward the dry creek bed before sinking into the dust. He knelt down beside the little rise pool, reflecting back at him from its dark, greenish depths. Lowering his head even further, he started to put his parched lips to the cool water, but then rose back to his knees.

He pulled the sharpened rock from his pouch—his brother's sacred object. He knew its history. It had been made by their grandfather, a great tool-maker. The point had never been used. Instead, it was kept for its great power, and luck. His brother had carried it everywhere—was never without it—but would never think of actually using it. It was too precious for that. The man turned the stone over and over in his hands, running his calloused fingers along its fine, intricately shaped edges. He put the stone to his face and pressed it there, hoping to absorb some of its energy. He knew he would need it.

He raised his hand and then gently lowered it, still cradling the stone, into the spring's rise pool. He turned his hand, opened his fingers, and watched as the fluted stone plunged downward, flashing the sun before sinking out of sight. The man lowered his head and wept as he drank deeply. He wept, because the beneficent Underworld Spirit wept for him. He closed his eyes tightly as he swallowed her salty tears.

ALMOST SEVEN-THOUSAND YEARS LATER, a man at a desk held the precious stone in his hands. He turned it over and over, running his fingers over its serrated edges. As he did, he mulled over what this find might mean. How did the stone end up in the spring? Why would someone put it in there? Surely it wasn't happenstance. It was hard for him to imagine such a finely worked piece accidentally finding itself buried in the throat of an ancient spring. The man put down the stone and picked up his pencil. He had some ideas.

Fifty years later, I interviewed this man—Bruce McMillan, a Professor of Anthropology at the University of Missouri. In the 1960s, in advance of the filling of Truman Reservoir, he had examined artifacts at springs in the Pomme de Terre valley. One of his theories about what Native Americans might have thought about springs derived from the finding of points, most of them in pristine condition, in these springs. They were buried in sediments in what McMillan calls "feeder conduits," the paths where water once rose to the surface at artesian springs. It seemed unusual to him to find unbroken, perfectly worked points in these feeders.

"You wouldn't think someone would just toss it in there, especially since it's pristine," McMillan told me. Rather, the act of tossing in the point, he surmises, probably shows some sort of sacrifice or gift to the spring spirit. These ancient people could very well have considered springs as sacred places; portals to the underworld. Such offerings might've also been made at larger springs, McMillan suggested, such as Big Spring, but they would've been quickly flushed out and buried in sediment.

Native Americans were no doubt attracted to springs. They needed drinking and bathing water, obviously, but also enjoyed a brisk plunge in the summertime or lounging in the coolness of a spring glen. They harvested food from spring branches and hunted game that was drawn there; or carried encrusted salt from saline springs back to their villages. At the larger springs, at least, especially ones near rock shelters, archaeologists have discovered numerous habitation sites and projectile points and even burial grounds.

It may have been especially important for people to inhabit areas near perennial springs during the warm, droughty, post-glacial period about 7,000 to 5,000 years ago, when many of Missouri's smaller streams dried up. Then, like now, springs tended to flow longer than surface streams, attracting game and providing water for domestic needs. McMillan points out that during the Dust Bowl era of the 1930s, when the Pomme de Terre River itself had dried up, these springs provided the only running water for miles around.

*Bennett Spring. Photo by Steve Spencer.*

But McMillan thinks there is even more to the story, so he keeps investigating—asking the questions. The story I related above—the men, the elk—is pure conjecture, of course, and probably never happened. But it could have. It is meant to make a point, and to raise new questions. Springs may no longer be sacred to us, but do we still need them? Why should we care what happens to them? Is the pollution or loss of a spring such a big deal? Does it have any real relevance to our lives?

I think that it does; but then I'm partial to springs. Like the man in my story, I find myself drawn to them. My earliest memories of springs is from camping with my family at Bennett Spring State Park. When my father had me rigged up for fishing, I immediately began searching for the spring, the source of the stream and, for that matter, the fish I was supposed to be catching. As I wandered upstream, casting clumsily, I suddenly came to a deep boiling pool of the most amazing azure blue. My imagination dipped into the mysterious underworld from which it rose, and never came out.

After college, when I began floating Missouri streams, I couldn't help but notice the many beautiful and magnificent springs. I bought Jerry Vineyard's book, *Springs of Missouri*, right after it came out in 1974, using it as a guidebook to locate obscure springs in the backcountry. Decades later, I became friends with Jerry, Missouri's original "cave man," and we talked about updating the spring book. It never happened, but the idea lingered.

I am still attracted to springs. I find my life enriched by them, even in small ways, as when I'm wade-fishing on a hot day and feel those little hidden springs—the pockets of extra-cold water suddenly tingling my feet—or the sight of a watercress-filled spring branch on a cold, gray day, glorious green against the dead brown of winter. But there is much more to springs than meets the eye, or the ears, or skin. For good reason, springs have been prized since the dawn of civilization, if not before. They have long been considered more than life-giving waters; they have been revered as living waters as well. That is the real story to be told here.

*The Author at Taberville Spring.*
*Photo by Beth Bullard.*

## HISTORICAL INTRODUCTION

JOHN POLK CAMPBELL TYPIFIED the restless frontier American of the early nineteenth century—ready to move on whenever new lands seemed to offer more promise or hope. Campbell grew up in the rolling country of Maury County, in central Tennessee. His people were farmers and hunters, scratching out an existence from the poor soils and wooded hills. In the fall of 1829, young John and his brother, Madison, saddled their horses and headed west, intending to find new homes for themselves and their families.

They crossed the Mississippi River and traveled due west through Arkansas Territory to Fayetteville, then northeast to Delaware Town, an Indian village on the James River in southwest Missouri, the "only place of note" in the area. They rode through the rippling Kickapoo Prairie and then probed further north into timbered land to the banks of a sparkling, spring-fed stream, a small tributary of the James River. There, on a low bluff over the stream, they found an unusual geologic feature—a slit in the rock, a natural well of "wonderful depth."[1]

They may have seen their reflections down in the well, or tossed in a large rock and listened to the deep "ker-plunk." In any case, it appeared to be a reliable and easily accessed water source. On the rising land south of the creek grew a stand of magnificent red oaks, signaling fertile soil. This, they determined, was what they had been looking for. With clearing, this upland area should yield healthy crops of corn. The cabin would be sheltered in the valley below but elevated above the creek's level of flooding. John carved his initials into a nearby ash tree before heading toward home.

The next February, John and his new wife, Louisa, with their baby not yet a year old, accompanied by six slaves and the Miller Family—husband, wife, and two children—set off on horses and in a wagon from central Tennessee—Missouri bound. They headed northward through Nashville on a decent road, then angled to the northwest through Hopkinsville, Kentucky, on worsening roads, to the Ohio River at Golconda, at the very southern tip of Illinois, where they crossed on a ferry. They proceeded due west through patches of prairie and woodlands to the Mississippi River and another ferry just north of Cape Girardeau, Missouri.

*Reed Spring Mill. Photo by Gayle Harper.*

This ferry was rickety and tipsy, and with the frigid winter gale, choppy water, and floating ice, they feared for their lives. They made it across, but from there the roads got even worse. They went westward through old Jackson, then angled northwest through the valley of the Whitewater River to Farmington, Missouri. Near this settlement, they may have seen a spring-powered sawmill on the headwaters of the Big River. This mill was no doubt busy producing sawed pine lumber for the St. Louis building boom when they passed through.

From Farmington, the party headed west to the little town of Caledonia, with twelve inhabitants, where they resupplied at a tiny store, the only one for miles around. In fact, there was very little "civilization" between here and the natural well where John had carved his initials, almost one-hundred fifty miles to the southwest as the crow flies.

West of Caledonia, where there was "scarcely any road," they plodded on to Steelville, where they may have taken on water at the big spring. They most certainly did that at Massey's Iron Works, twelve miles further west, where a huge spring surges below a towering bluff. They probably witnessed the beehive of activity at Massey's iron furnace and forges. This was Crawford County, which Alphonso Wetmore observed in 1837 had "the advantage of water-power sufficient to saw and grind the whole state of Missouri."[2]

Twelve miles further west they passed through Rolla, then on to the confluence of the Little Piney and Gasconade, where they stocked up on provisions at Harrison's Store, also serving as the post office for this lightly settled region. Twenty miles west from there, after crossing the Big Piney, they landed in Waynesville, where the huge Roubidoux Spring pours impressively from the ground. Had the travelers been here less than seven years later, in the winter of 1837, they would have seen a few hundred Cherokee camped here, resting on their forced march along the infamous "Trail of Tears."

From Waynesville, the little group turned to the southwest, up the valley of the Gasconade to its confluence with the Osage Fork, where they found a few white settlers, including "old Jim Campbell," the sheriff for "all of southwest Missouri." They crossed the Osage Fork and headed to Pleasant Prairie, now the town of Marshfield, before striking the James Fork about twenty miles east of the future town of Springfield. A few miles further west, at another large spring, they passed by Jerry Pearson's grist mill. They had finally arrived in Greene County, where large volumes of water "flow out of the earth, or break out in fissures of the rocks, of sufficient capacity to drive a pair of mill-stones."

*Arrow Rock Spring. Photo by Loring Bullard.*

From Pearson's mill, the band of travelers headed southwest into the tall blue grasslands, the Kickapoo Prairie. They rolled right on through the prairie and five miles beyond to the natural well, where they finally rested and camped on March 4, 1830. John Polk Campbell no doubt pointed out his tree-carved initials to the Burnett family, acquaintances of his from Tennessee, who in his absence over the last several months had built a rough cabin on the site. There is no mention in history books of how the issue was resolved, but Burnett withdrew to another site, John built his cabin at the natural well, and the rest, as they say, is Springfield history.

It had been a long, tiring journey for the Tennessee folks, following a somewhat circuitous route from their homes in Maury County to southwestern Missouri—a route largely dictated by water, in fact—the big rivers, at major crossings where ferries operated, and smaller rivers and springs, where settlements, stores, and mills had located, all connected by roads or at least traces, rough as they might be, and finally to their destination, the natural well, a never-failing spring. In the Missouri Ozarks, from Jackson to Springfield, the route largely meandered between mills and springs.

The Campbell party probably appreciated the intrinsic value of these springs to the growing civilization in the wilderness. One would think that they also admired the springs for their striking beauty. But at this stage of the state's development, at least, the emphasis was not on the beauty of springs, but their usefulness. "The value of these springs to the individuals who may secure title to them," Wetmore said, "is incalculable." What the Campbells did not see as they traveled through Missouri in 1830, and may not have known, was that many of the state's other springs were already being put to use in a variety of ways.

Saline springs, for example, lay just south and north of the Campbell's route in eastern Missouri, as well as further north and west. Henri Joutel, traveling with the French explorer LaSalle in 1687, wrote about salt springs near St. Genevieve and in 1700, Jesuit missionaries commented on salt-making operations at springs near the mouth of the Meramec River. By 1830, when the Campbells rolled across southern Missouri, salt had been made at Boone's Lick, near the Missouri River in central Missouri, for twenty-five years. Significant quantities of salt were also being manufactured by then in Ralls and Pike Counties.

Missouri springs were also being used for healing. The same year that Campbell arrived at the natural well to stake his claim, Bill Sublette purchased 800 acres near St.

*Spring Site at Liberty. Photo by Loring Bullard.*

Louis containing a pungent mineral spring. The strong sulfur smell of this spring was perceptible for quite a distance from where it plunged into the River des Peres in a stream "as big as your arm."[3] Sublette built a large, two-story stone guest house near the spring and by 1835 was running a fine watering place. By then, Isaac Van Bibber's tavern and boarding house at Loutre Lick Spring, forty miles west of St. Louis, had been servicing clients, including Thomas Hart Benton, for twenty years.

Unlike these salty or mineral-laden springs, most of Missouri's springs, especially those in the south part of the state, were clear, cool and good-tasting. Henry Schoolcraft, traversing southern Missouri in 1818-1819, often wrote in disparaging terms about the land he saw—calling it "sterile," "rough," and "barren"—but rejoiced at the quality of the springs he encountered, especially those along the North Fork River (what he called the "Limestone River"), gushing out "at almost every step from its calcareous banks." All of these springs were "remarkable for the purity of their waters." Elkhorn Spring, he wrote, possessed "the purity of crystal."[4]

Not long after Schoolcraft's tour, the largest of these springs were secured by millers for their power generating potential. But their pure, sweet waters were also considered the best drinking water available—better than wells, cisterns, or streams. Campbell no doubt noticed that springs had already influenced Missouri's settlement patterns, as he himself had a claim at the natural well. For Campbell and the state's other early inhabitants, a reliable water supply was a primary consideration when selecting a home site. Especially sought after were strong, perennially flowing springs issuing onto low bluffs or river benches—like the natural well—above the "malarias" of the flood-prone bottom-lands.

To these early settlers, springs were valuable personal property. Unlike a stream, the water of which usually flows through one's property before heading downstream to serve others, a spring—a compact, discrete point on the landscape—could actually be "owned." Landowners considered springs as essential amenities of desirable land. "I have a spring on my place that never runs dry" was commonly heard—a bragging right; a point of pride. A strong spring that "never ran dry" also carried an implied responsibility; during droughts owners were expected to share their precious water with their less fortunate neighbors.

The Campbells found that Missouri's large springs were connected by a ragged web of ruts and roads. Perennial springs a convenient distance apart along wagon roads served as stock watering and camping sites. The city of Blue Springs was organized around a series of springs used by westward-heading wagon trains and the big spring at Arrow Rock provided the first watering stop on the Santa Fe Trail south of the ferry across the Missouri River. Similarly, Cave Spring was one of the first stops westward from Independence on the California and Oregon Trails. Toll Gate Spring serviced the entrance to the Iron Mountain Road, and Pulltight Spring flowed at the bottom of a steep downhill section where teamsters had to "pull tight" on the reins.

The Campbells also saw many mills as they traversed the state, several of them using spring power to turn grinding stones or saw wood. In the eastern, more populated portions of Missouri, millers had already occupied many of the choice spring sites by the time the Campbells came through. These mills, in turn, became centers of social life, anchoring many of the state's nascent communities. For this and other reasons, over seventy villages, towns, or cities in the state now have the word "Spring" as part of their names.

At Massey's Iron Works in Crawford County, the Campbells saw the state's first iron works. The huge Maramec Spring powered these works through a series of water wheels that operated hammer mills and air blowers, as well as flour and grist mills. Other springs would find application as feed waters for woolen mills, tanneries, breweries, distilleries and canneries, and springs near railroad lines would become watering stops for steam-powered locomotives.

The Campbells no doubt saw springs as useful amenities. But eventually, their esoteric values were more widely appreciated. Springs would provide refreshingly cold water for swimming pools, fishing ponds and other recreational diversions at camps, resorts and lodges. Springs would also be used extensively for growing fish, replenishing the stocks of fish in the state's streams and supplying enthusiastic crowds of fishermen and women. Illustrating the importance of springs for fish propagation, almost all of the fish hatcheries and fish farms in Missouri are still located at springs.

Not long after the Campbells arrived in Missouri the state's expanding population began to exert deleterious effects upon its springs. Within forty years of the opening of Sublette's Sulphur Spring Resort on the River des Peres, encroaching development had gobbled up and destroyed the spring. The half dozen springs feeding into Chouteau Pond had also been obliterated by then. In Kansas City, springs at the original town site, their "veins laid bare" by street grading, had quickly dried up.[5] Most of the original springs in the center of Springfield no longer flowed or couldn't even be found by the end of the nineteenth century.

The Campbell's could not have imagined it, but some of the state's largest and most interesting springs have been lost. The Great Salt Spring in Saline County, once Missouri's largest saline spring—twenty-five feet deep, sixty feet in diameter and milky white in color—eventually filled with sediment washed from nearby farmed lands. Other springs, ironically, were submerged with water. A large spring, which a member of the 1806 Pike expedition described as "a most delightful basin of clear water, twenty-five paces of diameter," once flowed near the Osage River. The men bathed in it, finding it "deep and delightfully pleasant."[6] This spring, thought to have been Missouri's third largest, now lies below the quiet waters of the Lake of the Ozarks.

Springs in or near urban areas have been especially hard hit. Increasing numbers of wells lowered local water tables, reducing flows to nearby springs. Recharge areas were paved over, shutting off infiltration of rainwater feeding into the plumbing systems of springs. Other springs became polluted or otherwise unusable. We learned the hard way that springs are vulnerable to contamination and that, once polluted, can be very difficult to clean up.

Today, it seems—except for the magnificent blue giants at parks and along our scenic rivers—we largely ignore springs. And why not? Springs are no longer central to our lives, as they were in Campbell's time. We seldom use them for drinking water, and as energy sources they pale in comparison to big dams and coal or gas fired power plants. Long ago, food and milk were moved into real refrigerators. Old spring houses, no longer serving any useful purposes, have been bulldozed or left to fall into ruin. For the most part, people no longer see the loss or pollution of a spring as having particular relevance to their lives.

Kimberland Mill. Courtesy of History Museum for Springfield and Greene County.

That is a problem, because springs are more than just pretty places to visit. They are essential to the health of the land, and to its creatures, including us. At the very least, springs are sensitive barometers of groundwater quality, providing outward expressions of conditions hidden within the earth—conditions that we might not otherwise notice until it's too late, and that could negatively affect our deeper drinking water supplies. We need to understand springs in order to protect them, and thus, to protect our own interests.

But it is more than that. With good reason, springs have been prized and revered since the dawn of civilization, if not before. The Bible speaks often of them. Isaiah instructs believers to "joyously draw water from the springs of salvation." The inferences, the parallels are clear, given the confluence of pure, ever-flowing water with spiritual purity and everlasting life. In a very real sense, springs connect mankind to the essence of the good earth, a gift from and conduit to the hidden world beneath our feet. Springs should hold a special place in our minds, as well as our hearts.

Simply put—springs attract life, and always have. It is only natural for humans to be drawn to them, too, as John Polk Campbell was drawn to the natural well. But it is more than their breathtaking beauty or thirst-quenching waters that entice us. At a deeper level, springs can refresh, renew, and even inspire us. They are trusted, ever-faithful companions, serving up their living, life-giving waters with comforting consistency. This promise of everlasting water can even give us hope for the future.

## CHAPTER 1: ELIXIR OF THE GODS

JOHN POLK CAMPBELL'S DECISION to locate his cabin at the natural well was, in fact, very natural. In his time, springs were considered the best sources of drinking water available. A pure, sweet, never-failing spring was a miracle—a godsend, placed on this Earth by a beneficent Creator for mankind to find and use. A small spring could easily serve a household, but big springs could satisfy the needs of a village, or even a city. That is why Springfield citizens looked to the natural well as a potential public water supply long after Campbell was gone. In contrast, the well on the City Square, which had for decades been serving both horses and humans, often proved inadequate during droughts. As a better alternative, citizens eyed the natural well—the founding spring. After all, it was already being used to fill water carts to sprinkle the city's dusty streets.

At the urging of city council, local "mechanics" submitted a proposition to build the city a waterworks, with the natural well as the preferred source. As a test, these entrepreneurs inserted a "mammoth pump" in the natural well and pumped it hard. A city overseer pronounced it sufficiently productive. But some city leaders weren't convinced. They were skittish about technical details of the plan (e.g., would the water be used only for firefighting, or would mains be laid in the street for public use?), and suggested that large cisterns at the four corners of the square might be more practical.[1]

Most citizens, however, much preferred spring water over cistern water. Cisterns usually collected water off of roofs and could therefore contain leaves, bird droppings and, in the days before gas or electric heating, ashes and grit from wood or coal burning. As a result, cistern water often tasted stale and foul. When the cistern scheme was put forward at a council meeting, one Councilman suggested that people might be willing to pay for good spring water, but, he sneered, "who ever paid a cent for water from a cistern?"

The natural well did not become the city's public water supply. That honor went to Fulbright Spring, a larger source just north of town. In the summer of 1882, Paul Perkins of Geneseo, Illinois, owner of a waterworks construction company, came before Springfield's City Council with a plan. He would build the city a magnificent waterworks using Fulbright Spring as the water source. The water should be clean, Perkins stressed, as the spring was located in an area as yet "sparsely settled." Council must have been impressed with Perkins' plan and his depth of expertise, for they readily accepted the deal. But trouble arose even before Perkins had finished building the waterworks.

*Gathering at the Spring. Courtesy of History Museum for Springfield and Greene County.*          1

Some City Council members charged that Fulbright Spring was being fouled by outhouses in North Springfield, at the time a separate town. Council formed a committee to investigate, which they did by riding horses up the drainages above the spring, searching for signs of pollution. They also asked Professor Shepard of Drury College to conduct a "thorough microscopic examination" of the spring water. After his examination, Shepard pronounced the water "remarkably free from the animal and vegetable organisms which are so abundant in well and river waters."

*Fulbright Spring. Courtesy of City Utilities of Springfield Archives.*

In light of what we know today, this is a surprising statement. The recharge area for Fulbright Spring includes the South Dry Sac River, a losing stream. Water in this stream disappears underground at a series of swallow holes, or sinking points, and reappears at Fulbright Spring, about three miles to the west. A person can literally see, and hear, water draining out of the creek bed. Any tiny organisms in the stream could conceivably end up in the spring. And in the 1880s, before the water company used filtration or disinfection, these organisms quite possibly could have emerged alive from a customer's tap. But in 1884, council members deferred to Shepard, their local water expert.

The complacency was short-lived. Within two more years, the output of Fulbright Spring could barely keep up with the demands of the growing city. The water company looked for more water and found it at another spring, Jones Spring, where they built a brick pump house and forced spring water into mains using compressed air. Company officials breathed a sigh of relief, but before long customers began grumbling about the tap water's horrible taste. Some held up fruit jars of tap water "garnished with green moss" at Council meetings.

Professor Shepard was again asked to look into the matter. He examined the water of Jones Spring, this time finding "the presence of microbes in an alarming degree." Within one-hundred feet of the spring he saw an old mule pen used during the Civil War, its soil "impregnated to a high degree with excretory matter." City council demanded that the water company disconnect immediately from Jones Spring, which it did.

*VanDerhoefs at Pioneer Spring. Photo by Steve Spencer.*

A few more springs were added to the Springfield water system in the 1890s, but within a few years springs were largely phased out of the source portfolio. The company began drilling deep wells in 1915 and several decades later constructed two large reservoirs, providing vastly increased storage capacity. Springs fell out of favor as sources for public drinking water primarily because of their relatively small outputs, but also because they were so easily contaminated.

Fulbright Spring, however, is still in use. Today, Springfield is the only major city in Missouri using a spring for part of its municipal water supply. St. Louis and Kansas City use the big rivers flowing at their doorsteps, of course, but both of these cities once considered augmenting their water supplies with springs—Bennett Spring for Kansas City and Maramec Spring for St. Louis. In the early twentieth century, eleven cities in Missouri used springs as their primary sources for drinking water. All of these cities, except Springfield, now use sources other than springs, mostly deep wells.

While springs were being phased out for public water supplies, hundreds of homes in rural areas continued to use them. Some still do. Tom and Sharon VanDerhoef of Pioneer, Missouri, use a spring that tastes, they say, "wonderful—clear, clean, and crisp."[2] The spring flows from a white brick spring house through a watercress-choked channel toward Shoal Creek. The VanDerhoefs filter the water and use ultraviolet light for disinfection, because it doesn't affect the taste like chlorine might.

As I sat in their living room, overlooking the village of Pioneer, Tom explained the ingenuity behind their spring water system. It was designed by the millwright who once lived here. His engineering acumen resulted in a system that functioned nearly flawlessly for decades. Four-inch iron pipes ran downhill from the spring to a series of tanks or pits equipped with ram pumps. These pumps fed one-inch lines up to the top of the hill, far above the spring, where a large bell cistern provided gravity pressure to the homes below.

Near the spring sits the rusty remains of a ram pump. This simple device, nearly a perpetual motion machine, works on the principle of "water hammer;" that is, pressure waves ricocheting back and forth in an inclined drive pipe (see diagram). Because they have only a few moving parts, ram pumps last a long time. Along with the humming of mills, the characteristic "thud, thud, thud" of ram pumps could once be heard for considerable distances in the spring glens of Missouri.

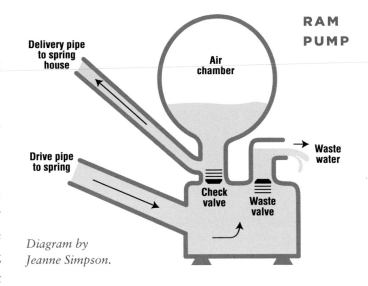

**RAM PUMP**

Delivery pipe to spring house

Air chamber

Drive pipe to spring

Waste water

Check valve

Waste valve

*Diagram by Jeanne Simpson.*

Before pumps became commonplace, a bucket was used to fetch spring water to the house. Rock, wood, or concrete basins were placed in excavated spring outlets to keep the water free of silt and leaves as it was being dipped out. Sometimes, in the early days, short sections of hollow tree trunks were used for this purpose, especially at springs welling up into floodplains or marshy areas. These trunk sections were called "gums" because gum trees seemed to work particularly well.

A bucket of water is heavy—25 to 50 pounds—so hauling it any distance was quite a chore. Where possible, pipes would be installed to convey spring water closer to the house. Nelle Allen, asked by a newspaper writer about her spring, remembered that someone had installed an iron pipe there, making it "easier for us oldies to get a cold drink without having to climb the slick hill." Like a lot of other folks, Nelle also drank directly from springs, lying on her stomach "like a puppy dog," although sometimes she had to "brush the water bugs back."[3]

Some Missourians were connoisseurs of spring water. Marcia Brown related to *Ozark Mountaineer* that her grandfather "loved cool spring water better than some folks love chocolate." Sunday drives for her family usually included at least one stop at a spring to collect a gallon or two to take home. Sometimes her grandfather would drive "a hundred miles out of his way to fill his jug," exclaiming proudly as he held it up, "Elixir of the Gods!"[4]

Belief in the healthful nature of spring water was widespread well into the twentieth century. A marker at Elm Spring in Greene County, placed in the 1930s, mentions early settlers in the area and then exhorts visitors to "take a drink of this pure water as a libation to the memory of those hardy pioneers." (Not mentioned are the outhouse and cemetery, located at the church directly

*Elm Spring, Greene County. Photo by Loring Bullard.*

above the spring.) Some of this belief in the purity of spring water survived until relatively modern times. Oz Hawksley, in his 1961 first edition of *Missouri Ozark Waterways*, advised readers that they could paddle right into Blue Spring on the North Fork River to "fill water jugs."

But even early in the nineteenth century, people generally understood that springs could become polluted under certain conditions—and that it was important to keep human sewage and animal wastes out of springs and other water sources. But the actual mechanisms of disease transmission were only partially understood. Creed Summers told *Bittersweet* that he once suspected his spring as a source of typhoid, but when he dug a tangle of roots out of the spring, "there was dead water-dogs in them roots. Well, that was the reason the water was filthy."[5]

In the twentieth century, the fear of disease led many people away from a reliance on springs as drinking water sources. Health experts increasingly warned people not to drink from springs unless the water had been disinfected. But other developments were probably more instrumental in making springs less attractive to homeowners. With advances in well drilling technologies, more and more people in rural areas turned to drilled wells. Electrification for pumps and deep wells with protective casings made home water supplies safer, more dependable, and easier to use.

Today, homeowners don't want to see anything in their drinking water. In the old days, when water was dipped from a spring basin or raised by a hand pump, critters would occasionally be seen in the water. Tiny white, almost translucent fish would sometimes appear in the bucket. When the natural well in Springfield was pumped, citizens saw fish, "even eels" in the water. Perhaps they were not surprised to find that these animals were attracted to the cool, delicious water of a spring. But they probably would have been surprised to learn that in the distant past, gigantic creatures had also been drawn to these same sparkling waters.

## CHAPTER 2: MR. KOCH'S SPRING

ALBERT KOCH INTENDED TO THRILL audiences at the house of curiosities he opened in St. Louis in 1836, located about where the Arch is today. Along with Egyptian mummies, Indian weapons and pipes, wax figures of Andrew Jackson and Santa Anna, stuffed birds and an Indian mummy from a cave in Kentucky, visitors could see a live bear and five alligators, all for the 25-cent admission price. The alligators fought each other, though, and one somehow fell out of a third story window, an accident described in a local paper under the headline, "Suicide." Regardless of these minor incidents, or maybe because of them, Koch attracted a steady stream of gawkers.[1]

In March 1840, as Koch lay in bed with a fever, word came from Benton County that a landowner had uncovered gigantic bones while building a mill at a spring. The site was near the "elephant lick" noted on a map drawn by Edward Clark, where Pierre Chouteau had unearthed remains of a prehistoric beast in about 1796.[2] This find, Koch thought, could produce important artifacts and an irresistible draw for his museum. Despite his illness, he was on a steamboat the next day ploughing up the rain-swollen Missouri River.

It took six days to reach the mouth of the flooded Osage River. There, Koch hired a guide with a small boat to take him twenty-four miles upstream on the Osage to its confluence with the Pomme de Terre River. He forded that river on a horse and continued another thirty miles to the spring site, where he booked a room at the cabin of the spring's owner, the postmaster of Hickory County. Koch remained there for four months while he conducted his dig.

According to a local legend, the Osage called the Pomme de Terre the "Big Bone River." The story, as Koch re-told it, goes like this: Large monsters invaded the region from the east, angering the resident animals. Red men dared not venture into the area to hunt. A great battle ensued between the animals and the monsters, resulting in many dead. The few surviving monsters continued westward. After the battle the Indians gathered up the casualties and burned them as a sacrifice. Koch no doubt repeated the legend because it added promotional value for his exhibits, as well as great copy for his museum literature.

However, the legend was remarkably similar to one documented by Thomas Jefferson in his *Notes on the State of Virginia* published in 1787. At Big Bone Lick, a marshy, spring-fed area along the Ohio River in Kentucky, huge bones strewn about the surface fueled speculation that strange creatures, what the Indians called "Big Buffalo," once inhabited the continent. These bones stirred the imagination of Thomas Jefferson, who wondered aloud if these beasts might still inhabit the West. In 1804 he instructed Lewis and Clark to be on the lookout for them.[3] In any case, Koch's "local" legend suspiciously paralleled the one related decades earlier by Jefferson.

The spring in Benton County welled up in a shady stand of tall oak and elm trees, appearing to "rise from the very

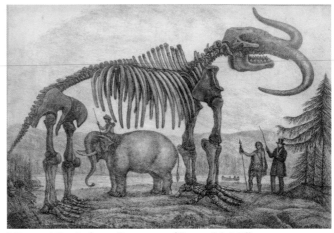

*Missouri Leviathan. Courtesy of Bruce McMillan.*

bowels of the earth." The flow seemed very stable, "never affected by the severest rain, nor did it become lower by the longest drought."[4] A boy had been cleaning out the spring opening when he discovered what looked like a very big tooth, inspiring further digging. Obviously, the postmaster had heard of Koch's interest in prehistoric remains and summoned him to the site, no doubt anticipating a hefty financial reward.

Koch was excited about big bones on the Pomme de Terre because he had recently excavated the remains of another large prehistoric beast at a spring along the Bourbeuse River. In October 1839, a farmer in Gasconade County (now Phelps County) uncovered these remains while trying to enclose a bad-tasting spring. Here, Koch found bones that he thought belonged to a clawed animal the size of an elephant. Further, the bones were lying in what looked like ashes, with several large rocks strewn nearby. Koch postulated that the animal had been killed with rocks by humans, who then roasted it.

A few months prior, Koch had gotten word of big animal remains at Sulphur Springs on the Mississippi River south of St. Louis. Here he found parts of two large skulls, along with many other bones, some of which would later be identified as belonging to extinct horses, ground sloths and a stag-moose. Koch took all of these bones to his museum where he tried to piece together what he had. The large skulls and massive leg bones must have come from a huge beast, one that he began to call his "Missouri Leviathan."[5]

Koch displayed the bones at his museum, including ten-foot-long tusks weighing 1,100 pounds each. The St. Louis *Argus* in July 1839 advised its readers that it would be "worth a journey of fifty

*Mastodon bones. Courtesy of Bruce McMillan.*

miles" to see the remains of the "huge animal discovered on the Herculaneum Road." But Koch still didn't have enough bones to fashion a complete skeleton for his exhibit, so the summons from Benton County in 1840 was particularly welcomed.

At the Benton County spring, Koch placed platforms of walnut logs down in the muck in an attempt to keep his men dry as they worked. Soon, some very exciting finds came to light, including a massive, largely intact skull. Koch carefully packed up the fossils, intending to float them down the Pomme de Terre on a raft made of four hollowed out walnut logs. But the river was too low. Instead, he hired three wagons, each pulled by four oxen, and made his way with this slow-moving caravan over the rough roads to Boonville, where he loaded his precious cargo onto a steamboat bound for St. Louis.

Later that year, Koch felt he had enough bones from multiple digs to assemble a full skeleton for display at his museum. With the benefit of hindsight, many people today would say the reconstructed creature looks awkward, or even grotesque. It was certainly impressively sized—thirty-two feet in length and fifteen feet high. The tusks curved backwards, resembling a giant handle-bar mustache. Koch remarked that the tusks were so situated in the head that it would be "utterly impossible for him to exist in a timbered country." The beast no doubt inhabited water-courses, he said, since its feet were webbed. He envisioned it as being similar to a hippo, walking on the bottom of riverbeds, rising occasionally to take air. There was some resemblance to the mammoths recently unearthed in other regions, and Koch conceded that his Leviathan could be "some extinct mammoth of the waters, as the behemoth was of the land," a reference to the Biblical beast described in the book of Job.

Koch exhibited the Leviathan at his St. Louis museum, initially generating great public excitement, but his frequent absences on fossil-hunting trips eventually led to a decline in attendance. He decided to explore bigger venues, so he sold his museum in 1841 and took the Leviathan on the road—New Orleans, Louisville, Philadelphia. But scientists in the natural history hotbed of Philadelphia scoffed at Koch's reconstruction. They said the bones were assembled incorrectly; that they actually came from several different animals; and that most of them actually belonged to an extinct animal already described, the American mastodon.

Koch was undeterred. He took his mounted skeleton to Europe, exhibiting it in London and Dublin. In 1843, he sold it to the British Museum for 1,300 pounds. British scientists promptly re-assembled the beast in a more correct manner. This re-constituted, down-sized American mastodon went on display at the British Museum, where it resides today.[6]

Koch's claim of finding Indian artifacts in association with mastodon remains and even suggesting that humans had killed the animal angered many people, including scientists. Most scholars at the time didn't believe Indians had been around that long, and claims that they had co-existed with "antediluvian beasts" like mastodons were preposterous. But many years later at Kimmswick, Koch would finally be vindicated when scientists uncovered definitive proof that humans had indeed killed mastodons—the discovery of a Clovis projectile point, at least 10,000 years old, in close association with mastodon remains.[7]

Another man who has found mastodon remains at Koch's Spring is Bruce McMillan, Professor of Anthropology at the University of Missouri. The gray-haired, soft spoken McMillan spent twenty years as curator of the Illinois Museum of Natural History. His archaeological work in Missouri extends back to the 1950s, including excavations at several springs in Benton and Hickory Counties. He worked at Koch's Spring in the 1960s, as Truman Reservoir began to fill.

As we sat in his office in Columbia, snow blowing sideways outside, I asked McMillan if a person could visit Koch's spring today. It would be difficult, he said, since it is covered by the waters of Truman Reservoir. McMillan was proud of the fact that he had found the famous spring before the reservoir filled. It wasn't shown on any map and was overgrown with trees and brush. He had been guided by Koch's description of an anvil-shaped rock near the spring, which luckily McMillan's team had located. In the spring sediments, they discovered some of the original walnut platforms used by Koch's diggers.[8]

Some of the other springs in the vicinity—Trolinger, Jones, Kirby—have also yielded mastodon remains, along with an assortment of other animals. McMillan and his team discovered that Kirby Spring had been excavated not long after Koch's time. Koch's success, McMillan conjectured, had apparently created "a real bone rush," and "everybody was aware that Koch had been able to sell that mastodon skeleton to the British museum." Regardless, McMillan's team pulled many amazing artifacts from these slowly seeping springs.

Such springs are biological treasure troves. Because of the low oxygen content and acidic nature of spring and bog mucks, bones and durable plant parts are wonderfully preserved. Pollen grains and animal remains at Trolinger Spring indicate that 32,000 to 25,000 years ago, when

*Mastodon mandible. Courtesy of Bruce McMillan.*

mastodons and musk oxen roamed the floodplain, the vegetation was primarily open grassland with scattered pines. Fast forwarding 10,000 years, the pine lands had become a dense spruce forest, inhabited by ground sloths and giant beavers in addition to mastodons.[9]

I knew I would never see Koch's spring, but I wanted to at least visit a spring in the same area that had yielded mastodon remains. After some searching using McMillan's hand-drawn map, I finally located Jones Spring. It was more like a pond. The spring water was greenish but crystal clear, and I could see a deep area in the bottom where McMillan's crew had excavated. It seemed odd to me that a place so famous in archaeological circles would be unmarked, unmolested, sitting quietly in its overgrown floodplain. I also had to wonder: what attracted the mastodons to this place?

It may have simply been the water, or the lush vegetation around it. It might also have been what was in the water. At Kimmswick, south of St. Louis, the springs were slightly saline. Salty water attracts many kinds of beasts, especially the hoofed variety—bison, elk, deer—which eagerly lick the salt-encrusted soil around the spring. In fact, salty springs were once called "licks" for this reason. The saltiness may have been what attracted the mastodons to Kimmswick and to Big Bone Lick in Kentucky, and maybe to the springs along the Pomme de Terre.[10]

People need and crave salt too. There is ample evidence that Native Americans collected salt at springs in Missouri, and several of the state's saline springs were once the sites of commercial salt-making operations. Along with lead mining and fur trapping, saltworks were among the state's earliest commercial enterprises. In the early nineteenth century, a saltworks near the Missouri River was operated by one of the state's most prominent frontier heroes—a man who, in spite of the considerable risks, saw financial promise in the "licks."

## CHAPTER 3: BOONE'S LICK

WHEN I VISITED BOONE'S LICK in December 2017, the tired old spring wasn't even flowing. It had been a dry year up until then, so the lack of flow wasn't unexpected, but still disappointing. It's hard to believe that this little seep could have ever supported a major commercial enterprise; or that it could've played such a significant role in opening up western Missouri to settlement; or that men would've risked their lives to work here. It's hard to believe because the commodity once produced here is now so mundane and cheap that we throw it by the bucketful on our walks, steps, and driveways just to melt the ice—it is common salt.

Of course, things were a lot different in the early days of the western frontier. Salt was a necessity and in high demand—primarily for curing meat to last through long winters. It took about four pounds of salt to preserve a twenty-pound ham. Large quantities of salt were also used in curing hides. Luckily, there was a "fair sprinkling" of salt springs in the western country, placed there, traveler Fortescue Cuming suggested in 1810, "by an all bountiful nature, or rather by Nature's God, for supplying both the intellectual and brute creation with an article so necessary to both, in the heart of an immense continent, so remote from any ocean."[1]

The earliest European explorers in Missouri noted that Indians had been harvesting salt at saline springs near St. Genevieve. By the Mississippian period, about twelve hundred to four hundred years ago, Native Americans had become more agricultural, growing maize, squash and beans. A plant-based diet contains much less salt that a meat-dominated one. This could explain why so many ancient pottery sherds are found at Missouri's salt springs—Native Americans were collecting it to take back to their villages.[2]

By 1700, salt-making camps were in operation near St. Genevieve and at the mouth of the Meramec River. These were small-scale operations, each utilizing only a few workers.[3] Much larger saltworks existed in the eastern U.S. before 1800, but they were hundreds of miles from Missouri. To supply Missouri's pioneers, salt had to be shipped westward by boat, greatly increasing its cost. Thus, salt-making on the frontier became an enticing commercial opportunity. Missouri's most famous pioneer family, the Boones, with their salt-making experience and frontier skills, were uniquely positioned to take advantage of this opportunity.

In the spring of 1799, Nathan Boone helped move his aging parents from their farm on the Little Sandy River in Ohio to a Spanish land grant on the Femme Osage, forty miles west of St. Louis. Nathan's brother Morgan had already scouted out the area and built a cabin. Nathan grew up there, spending much of his youth roaming the backwoods just as his father had done in Kentucky. He

*Boone's Lick Site ca. 1890, from* Report on Mineral Waters, *by Paul Schweitzer.*

went on long hunts with his childhood companion, Matthias Van Bibber. As they became more proficient hunters and trappers, they expanded their forays farther and farther from home.[4]

In the fall of 1804, the pair worked their way far to the west, into what is now Kansas, trapping beaver and other fur-bearers on the headwaters of the Grand River. They had knowingly encroached well into the territory of the Osage, who jealously guarded their furs. Early one morning a party of Osage hailed Boone's camp, where about five dozen pelts were stacked. The Indians scolded the men and took their furs and horses. Another party was searching for them, the Osage warned, and they advised the young trappers to head home.

Sure enough, the second party of Osage caught up with the two men after they shot at a deer. This group was more belligerent. Nathan told them he worked for the Chouteau brothers, prominent fur traders the Indians undoubtedly knew, but the Osage probably didn't believe him. The Indians demanded the pair accompany them. When they resisted, an Indian hit Nathan on the head with a rifle ramrod, raising a large knot. Nathan kept his cool and the Indians finally agreed to leave if the trappers gave up most of their lead and powder. The Indians left with their booty, but not before also relieving the men of their blankets.

Afoot, with little powder and few bullets left, the two men had little choice but to start walking home, a few hundred miles to the east. The weather turned bitterly cold. They trudged through knee-deep snow, crossed the Missouri River on ice, and slept in caves when they could. With

*Remains of Salt Well at Boone's Lick. Courtesy of Missouri State Parks.*

the extreme cold, their rifles wouldn't shoot straight. They had only five bullets between them, and their hands were shaking so badly they could hardly sight their rifles. Surviving mostly on wild grapes, they only had meat because they managed to kill a cougar in an abandoned house, skinning the cat to make furry vests.

Finally, they came upon a hunter's camp. The men there gave the freezing, bedraggled trappers food and new moccasins, probably saving their lives, as they were still over a hundred miles from home. Along this last leg the half-frozen pair came upon a small spring not far from the east bank of the Missouri River, where they paused to drink. The water was salty, they noted, but they drank freely anyway. Right then or maybe soon afterwards, a germ of an idea formed in Nathan's mind—a new business opportunity, perhaps.

When he got home, Nathan presented the idea to his father. How about a salt-making operation at the spring he had discovered? To supplement the family income, he said, he would make salt in the summer, when furs were of low quality anyway. Daniel, however, having manufactured salt at the Blue Licks in Kentucky in 1778, knew full well the dangers and hardships. He had been captured by Shawnee Indians and had barely escaped. More recently, several saltworks on the Missouri frontier had been attacked by Indians; some salt-makers had been killed. So not surprisingly, Daniel tried to dissuade his son from the enterprise.

But Nathan would not be deterred. In the late spring of 1805, he led a half-dozen men on horses heavily laden with large iron kettles, pans, shovels, and axes back to the salty spring. The men cut and stacked firewood, gathered rocks for the construction of furnaces, and fashioned troughs from hollowed out half-logs to convey spring water to the kettles. They constructed a wooden, human-powered wheel to raise water from the spring to the log flumes. The kettles sat on ledges atop the furnaces, held in place with daubs of clay. Fires were stoked and burned night and day. When most of the water in the kettle had boiled away, the men ladled out the bottom deposits, called bittern, and dried it further in shallow pans. In this way, they made about twenty-five to thirty bushels of salt per day, boiling away 15,000 to 18,000 gallons of spring water in the process.[5]

*Portion of Saltworks Diorama, Arrow Rock State Historic Site. Courtesy of Missouri State Parks.*

The salt was packed in barrels and sent down the Missouri River in flatboats and keelboats to St. Louis, where it fetched about $2 to $2.50 a bushel. Within a few years, the work force at Boone's Lick had expanded to about twenty men, producing over 100 bushels of salt a day. As the woodchoppers whittled away at the forests around the spring, they had to go farther and farther for wood until, a geologist later noted, four square miles around the saltworks had been "denuded of timber."[6]

Within a few years of starting the saltworks, Boone began pursuing other interests, spending more and more time working as a surveyor and army guide. At the saltworks, Indians stole oxen and cattle that had strayed too far. Profits sagged. By 1811, Boone had had enough. He sold his shares in the business to his partner, James Morrison. Tragically, Morrison's son, sixteen year-old Joseph, was scalded to death in a vat of boiling water. But except for the war years of 1812 to 1815, the saltworks remained in operation for another thirty years.

By the time Nathan Boone got out of the salt-making business, the price of salt had already started to fall. With bigger springs and stronger brines, major Eastern saltworks could vastly out-produce small operations like Boone's. Onondaga, in upstate New York, was turning out over one million bushels of salt annually by 1810. But Boone's biggest competitor at the time was the Kanawha Saltworks, in what is now West Virginia, which at its peak had thirty furnaces in operation, fired with coal mined nearby. This, plus the availability of local slave labor kept production costs low. These operations made serious inroads into the Missouri market.

Missouri's saltworks got a little boost in 1821, when the enabling legislation for statehood stipulated that large tracts of land around salt springs be reserved for the use or control of the state. Within four years, 11,000 acres near salt springs had been set aside. But Missouri salt was dealt another blow when the Erie Canal, the "ditch that salt made," was completed in 1825, allowing Onondaga salt to flood the interior. This salt had become Missouri's best seller by the 1840s. In the 1840s and 1850s, steamboats brought even cheaper salt to Missouri from Cape Cod, the Bahamas, and even Liverpool, England. Missouri saltworks had no hope of competing with these major sources, and locally produced salt had largely faded from the scene by the mid-nineteenth century.[7]

At Boone's Lick, now a state historic site, the remains of the furnaces can still be seen, as can a wooden surface casing from a well drilled in 1869 in hopes of reaching stronger brines. At one point, someone even attempted to raise oysters in the salty water. In the visitor center at Arrow Rock State Historic Site, across the Missouri River from Boone's Lick, a diorama depicts Boone's salt-making camp. In a nearby glass case sits the massive wooden axle of the water-wheel that was used to raise spring water to the overhead flumes.

Saline springs made salt production possible, but these unique geologic features possessed other virtues. In the nineteenth century, salty spring water was considered healthful to drink or to bathe in. This idea generated a wholly different kind of enterprise. By the time Boone began making salt in 1805, "taking the waters" had become a popular trend nationally. Resorts offering mineral water drinking and bathing "cures" had popped up in many scenic locations in the East. Promoters of these places had convinced a fickle public that taking the waters was not only healthful—it was fashionable. Another Missouri pioneer watched these trends with interest and decided to capitalize on a strong-smelling spring very near to his home town.

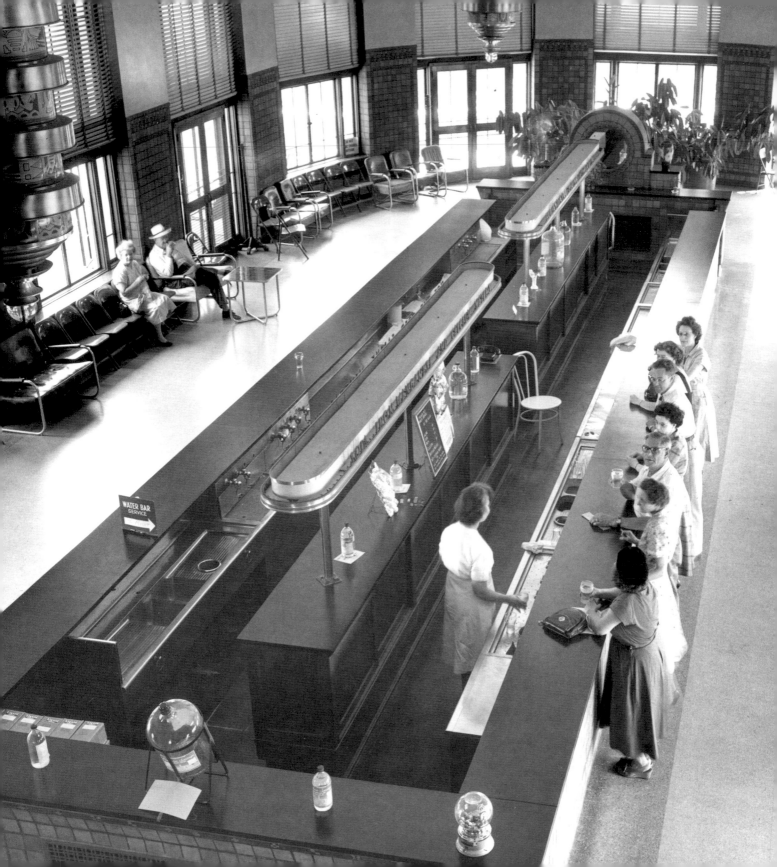

WATER BAR
SERVICE →

## CHAPTER 4: HEALING SPRINGS

THE FUR TRADE DOMINATED commercial enterprises on the upper Missouri River in the 1820s, and most of this business and the furs it produced funneled through St. Louis. Young Bill Sublette of St. Charles watched this thriving industry with interest, and in 1822 he signed up for a western trapping expedition under William Ashley, fur baron and Lieutenant Governor of Missouri. From this start, Sublette went on to make a name for himself, first as a "mountain man" and later as a fur trader and businessman. He pioneered one of the major routes on the Oregon Trail and drove the first team of wagons to reach the Santa Fe trade. These enterprises made him wealthy.[1]

Sublette planned to settle down in the St. Louis area. In 1830, he bought almost 800 acres of land on the River des Peres, near St. Louis, for $7,000. This parcel became known as the "Sulphur Springs" tract, because an odorous spring gushed out of the riverbank on the property. Major Stephen Long's western expedition passed through in 1818 and Edwin James, the group's biologist, commented that the spring emitted "a strong sulfurous odor perceptible at one-hundred yards." Sublette knew there was something special about this spring, since James had already noted that cattle and horses "came daily in great numbers, from distant parts of the prairie, to drink it."[2] Sublette also knew about the fashionable watering places of the East, like White Sulphur Springs in Virginia, which had become immensely popular. He sensed that a business like that might go over well in St. Louis.

He had good reason to be optimistic. Belief in the healing powers of mineral springs was widespread, with deep Biblical roots. The Bible references Siloam's pool, a healing spring and part of Jerusalem's water supply, where Jesus gave a blind man sight, and the pool of Bethesda, with its five columned porticoes, where the waters would heal when "troubled" by angels. These ideas played well into the hands of mineral water promoters. Reverend Claudius Buchanan, preaching at a mineral water resort in 1811, said "the same power, which gave virtue to the well of Bethesda, hath opened the fountain of health in this place."[3]

With this as a background, and promoters beating the drums, resorts featuring healing springs proliferated in America. By 1830, spa touring had become all the rage along the eastern seaboard, with people traveling long distances to drink and bathe in medicinal waters. They flocked to resorts in the mountains, at least partly to escape the heat, humidity and "miasmas" of the low-lying coasts. Medical practitioners touted the healing virtues of mineral springs, which worked hand-in-hand with the restorative powers of rest and relaxation offered at resorts. The most coveted medicinal waters, of course, were those with high mineral contents, tasting salty or bitter or smelling of sulfur—in other words, containing all the indications of "good medicine."

*White Sulphur Springs. Author collection.*

Sublette's spring seemed to have the right nauseating qualities. A visitor claimed that it tasted like the "peculiar washings of a gun barrel."[4] Sublette sent samples of his spring water to St. Louis for examination and was delighted to learn that its chemical signature resembled that of Virginia's White Sulphur Spring. In the spring of 1835, he began working on a large, two-story stone guest house near the spring that would accommodate sixty boarders. Within three years of opening, the Sulphur Spring Resort had earned a wide reputation as a fine watering place. Sublette even provided a nine-pin bowling alley and horse track, both illegal in St. Louis at the time.

Sublette died in 1845, having long suffered from the effects of consumption (apparently not cured by the water of his own spring). The Sulphur Springs property sold three years later. After that, the resort suffered a gradual decline, and by the 1870s was in near ruin. By this time, the River des Peres had become an open sewer, contaminated by sewage and runoff from St. Louis, and the old guest house finally burned. The gradual, sad decline of Sulphur Spring is a story retold at a number of mineral-spring resorts that once graced the Missouri landscape.

One of these, Missouri's earliest mineral spring resort, was Loutre Lick, fifty miles west of St. Louis. Nathan Boone obtained the land containing the pungent spring in about 1800 and attempted salt-making, but the enterprise failed. By 1815 he had sold the land to Isaac Van Bibber, whom Daniel Boone had raised like a son from the age of three. Van Bibber constructed a rambling tavern and boardinghouse at Loutre Lick that became a legendary watering hole. It served as a popular way station on the Boone's Lick Road, which carried stage service between St. Louis and Fort Osage, a distance of 273 miles.

*Van Bibber Tavern. Courtesy of Missouri State Historical Society.*

Daniel Boone's other son, Daniel Morgan, settled at Loutre Lick in 1819. Daniel senior visited and drank the spring water, seeking relief for a kidney ailment. Washington Irving stopped by, promising that if he ever got rich, he'd build a home there. And Thomas Hart Benton visited frequently, bragging about his personal "Bethesda" in the halls of Congress in Washington.

Loutre Lick declined before the Civil War but was revived in the 1880s, when it was redeveloped and renamed Mineola. The water was bottled and sold widely and, as the *Montgomery County Leader* gushed in 1916, "quite a sprinkle of pure-hearted and interesting maiden ladies and handsome widows" frequented the place. When I visited the site in 2000 there were no maidens or handsome widows about, just a weathered old pagoda standing over the smelly, weakly flowing spring.

Another resort that boomed and then faded is Chouteau Springs in Cooper County, a place which entwined two other St. Louis fur barons—William Ashley and Pierre Chouteau, son of St. Louis founder Pierre de Laclede. In appreciation of Chouteau's honesty in fur trading, Osage Indians in 1792 presented him with a huge land grant along the Missouri River. The tract included valuable salt springs on the Lamine River, and the large expanse of forested land included in the grant was intended, in part, to secure wood for salt-making furnaces.

Because of imprecise surveys and legal descriptions, Chouteau had trouble perfecting the title to his land. It took the help of fellow St. Louisan William Ashley, who had been appointed by Congress to register preemption claims, to shepherd Chouteau's claim through Congress. For his assistance, Ashley received one-fourth of the land. This piece contained a prominent mineral spring, which Ashley named in Chouteau's honor.

Ashley died in 1838 and was buried atop an old Indian mound in St. Louis. He left his huge estate to his wife and daughters, who, in turn, sold part of it containing the mineral spring, which the new owners developed into a health resort. The enterprise, going strong

*El Dorado Springs. Courtesy of Missouri State Historical Society.*

in the 1850s, declined during the Civil War, but by the 1880s had recaptured its former glory. A magnificent eighty-foot wide drive coursed through the nearly 200 platted residential lots, which sold from $50 to $100 each. The spring water, with its "light and agreeable taste," was said to compare favorably with Saratoga Springs in New York. The resort featured a spring-fed swimming pool, bath houses, bowling alley, billiard hall, and "good dry tenting grounds, free from annoyances."[5]

The Chouteau Springs resort had a good long life, finally closing to public use in 1962. I visited the site in 1998 and again in 2018. Nothing much had changed in the intervening two decades. The old spring still flows, welling up greenish-black inside a buried tile, belching gas bubbles, pink and white bacterial slimes wafting in the current. The old swimming pool is also still there, its walls crumbling, its floor covered with a luxuriant stand of cattails. Except for the distant thundering of I-70, an eerie quiet now surrounds the place.

These ruins of once-thriving resorts are reminders of the boom-and-bust nature of the mineral spring resort business. At their peaks in the nineteenth century, these places were high points on

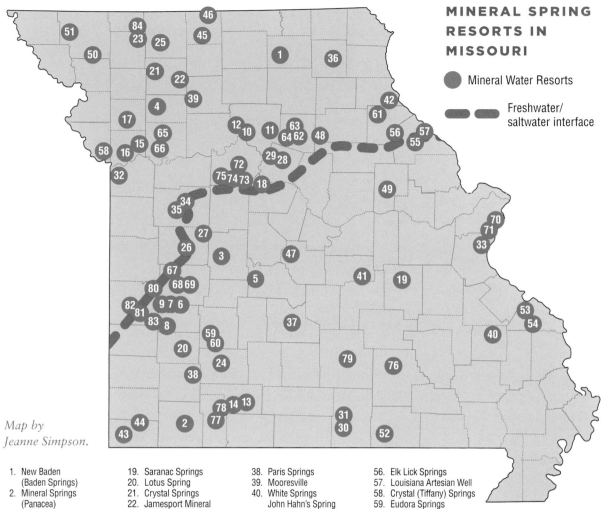

# MINERAL SPRING RESORTS IN MISSOURI

⬤ Mineral Water Resorts

▬ ▬ Freshwater/saltwater interface

*Map by Jeanne Simpson.*

1. New Baden (Baden Springs)
2. Mineral Springs (Panacea)
3. White Sulphur Springs
4. Bonanza Spring
5. Climax Springs
6. Cedar Springs
7. El Dorado Springs
8. Jerico Springs
9. Nine Wonders (West El Dorado)
10. Brunswick Mineral Well
11. Salisbury Well
12. Triplett Well
13. Eau de Vie
14. Reno
15. Excelsior Springs
16. Reed Springs
17. Plattsburg Mineral Spring
18. Chouteau Springs
19. Saranac Springs
20. Lotus Spring
21. Crystal Springs
22. Jamesport Mineral Springs
23. Siloam Springs
24. Bethesda Springs
25. Heilbron Spring
26. Clinton Artesian Well
27. Windsor Medical Well
28. Fayette Salt Spring
29. Glasgow Mineral Spring
30. Dixon (Cure-All) Springs
31. Siloam Springs
32. Young's Medical Well
33. Montesano Springs
34. Colbern (Electric) Springs
35. Pertle Springs
36. Forest Springs
37. Lebanon Magnetic Well
38. Paris Springs
39. Mooresville
40. White Springs John Hahn's Spring Mineral Well
41. Vichy
42. Vernette Mineral Well
43. Galbraith's Medical Well
44. Indian Springs
45. Bowsher Mineral Spring
46. Lineville Mineral Well
47. Aurora Springs
48. Harris Springs
49. Mineola
50. Barnard Medical Well
51. Burlington Junction Mineral Spring
52. El Dorado Springs
53. Lithium Springs
54. Schumer Springs
55. B.B. Spring
56. Elk Lick Springs
57. Louisiana Artesian Well
58. Crystal (Tiffany) Springs
59. Eudora Springs
60. Graydon Springs
61. Spalding Springs
62. Radium Spring
63. Randolph Spa
64. Randolph Springs
65. Mineral City
66. St. Cloud
67. Appleton City Well
68. Monegaw Springs
69. Salt Creek Spring
70. Belcher's Artesian Well
71. White Sulphur Springs
72. Blue Lick Springs
73. Elk Lick Springs
74. McAllister Springs
75. Sweet Springs
76. Welch Spring
77. Galena Medical Spring
78. Ponce de Leon
79. Blankenship Medical Springs
80. Fair Haven (Conely Springs)
81. Greene Springs
82. Nevada Artesian Well (Lake Park White Sulphur Spring)
83. Zodiac
84. Fairview Mineral Spring (Denver Bathhouse)

Missouri's social landscape, frequented by the fashionable elements of society as well as health-seekers. Over ten decades, from the 1830s to the 1930s, spring-based resorts popped up over much of the state, with about eighty mineral spring sites eventually hosting resorts, although for some of them the term "resort" might be a bit of a stretch (see map).

The locations of Missouri's mineralized springs and resorts conform to a recognizable geologic pattern. The freshwater-saltwater interface, a line separating the fresh, or "sweet" springs of the Ozarks

*Climax Spring. Photo by Loring Bullard.*

from the more heavily mineralized springs to the north and west, arcs across the state from southwest to northeast (see map). Many of the state's famous mineral spring resorts—such as Eldorado Springs, Pertle Springs, Sweet Springs, Blue Lick Springs, McAllister Springs, Chouteau Springs, Randolph Springs, and Spalding Springs—were situated near this line.

In 1892, Paul Schweitzer of the Missouri Geological Survey published a book on Missouri's mineral springs. He tested the water of many of them and found that they compared favorably with the famous spas of Europe. Given sufficient development and promotion, Schweitzer suggested, Missouri's springs, possessing "virtues of a very high order," could become famous "far beyond the confines of the state."[6] In spite of Schweitzer's optimism, however, many of Missouri's mineral spring resorts were already in decline by 1900, and most were gone by the 1920s.

Of the eighty mineral spring resorts that once existed, only one remains in business today— Excelsior Springs near Kansas City, where one can still drink at the "world's longest water bar" or relax in a hot mineral water bath. All of the rest are gone. Of course, many of them never rose to any degree of prominence in the first place. Hardly anyone remembers the names of the more obscure resorts, each of which, at one time, dreamed of becoming another Excelsior Springs—places like Bowsher, Lotus, Elk Lick, Graydon, Balm, Arnica, Cure-All, Electric Springs and Zodiac.

*Jerico Springs. Photo by Loring Bullard.*

By the early part of the twentieth century, the public had largely turned to other sources for personal health—primarily the mainstream medical profession. They were also looking for more exciting leisure pursuits—vacations and sporting events, for example. A long stay at a mineral water spa, with its methodical drinking and bathing regimens, no longer appealed to fast-paced lifestyles. For mineral spring resorts, the handwriting was clearly on the wall. Missourians were looking for hydration and good taste rather than medicine in their drinking water.

With the demise of resorts, mineral springs were no longer in demand. Most of them were too small to produce power or to support major commercial or industrial enterprises. For profitable investments, businesspeople sought big, powerful springs—more flow, greater heads of fall. These attributes were important because they determined a spring's ability to do work. And many people believed that unused, free-flowing springs—those doing no work at all—represented valuable economic resources going to waste.

## CHAPTER 5: SPRINGS AT WORK

A SPRING TUMBLING DOWN A HILLSIDE is a serene and beautiful sight, its gurgling flow melodious and soothing. But, at least in days past, that cascading water represented raw power—the roaring a shout of opportunity. After all, idle springs could be put to work doing something useful. Of particular interest were a spring's volume of flow and its "head of fall," the vertical distance between the spring outlet and the valley floor below. These factors determined the power that a spring could generate. Power meant business potential and, more importantly, profits. Millers were among the first to take advantage of this opportunity—and to tap into a free source of energy.

Samuel Greer was one of Missouri's early millers. He left Tennessee in 1859 with his father, John, and settled in Oregon County. Thirty year-old Samuel built the family's first grist mill below the spring in 1860. After serving in the Confederate Army, he returned home to find that bushwhackers had burned the mill. He rebuilt it as a three-story structure that extended out over the spring branch, where he installed a turbine for power. But the mill had a major drawback. The road down to it was treacherously steep, making it difficult for heavily loaded wagons to negotiate. Further, Greer had wanted to build a larger mill, but there wasn't enough room in the narrow valley bottom.[1]

So, in 1883 Greer dismantled his mill and hauled the timber and milling machinery to the top of the hill, where he built a large new roller mill. At the same time, he repaired and strengthened the old mill dam on the spring branch, far below. But tragedy struck when his 23 year-old son, Lewis, was killed by a falling timber while working on the dam. Samuel blamed himself, since he had persuaded Lewis, who had wanted to move to Oregon, to stay and help with repairs. With Lewis's death, all work stopped for a month, and Lewis's new bride, suddenly a widow, never again went near the dam.

Greer finally got back to the project, devising an ingenious solution to get power from the spring to the top of the hill. He used a long cable looped over pulleys suspended on iron towers, driven from the turbine at the dam. Engineers told him the complicated mechanism wouldn't work, and it did take him a long time to fine-tune it, but he finally got it fully functional in 1899. But Greer was almost seventy by then. He sold the mill to his partner, George Mainprize, and not long afterward, in 1904, sold the rest of his land. The old roller mill still stands at the top of the hill, near Highway 19, and preservationists are trying to save the historic structure. A new trail has been built down to the beautiful spring, Missouri's second largest, boiling up from the riverbed. But at the spring, there are hardly any signs of the original mill, dam, or other infrastructure; just a few rusting, twisted cables snaking through the weeds. Like most of Missouri's old spring-powered mills, this one is but a memory.

Mills were once thickly set in the valleys of Missouri, providing essential services to the populace. It helped that early millers had the support of government. Passed by the Missouri legislature shortly after the state's formation in 1821, "mill acts" encouraged the establishment of water-powered mills as a recognized "public good."[2] These

*Greer Mill. Photo by Steve Spencer.*

statutes allowed a miller to dam a spring or river as long as he owned the property, even if it was only on one bank, and he could even back water onto adjacent properties. He had only to petition the county court, which would assess any potential damages to neighbors and determine the amount of compensation to be paid.

Springs offered distinct advantages over rivers for the operation of mills. Rivers sometimes flooded and at other times had very low flows, both of which limited their usefulness. Springs, in contrast, had lower but more consistent flows, extending run times and limiting damages. Further, the constant temperatures of springs prevented the formation of machinery-obstructing ice in the wintertime. But milling in spring country also presented certain engineering challenges. When a mill dam was built at Big Spring in Lawrence County, water wouldn't raise to the desired height behind the dam because it leaked out through another spring. This was a very common problem. Millers attempted to plug leaks behind their dams with rocks, sediment, or concrete.

By the end of the 1800s, hundreds of water-powered mills—grist mills, flour mills, carding mills, sawmills—had sprung up across Missouri, a large number of them at springs. The earliest mills were built near population centers in the eastern part of the state. There were at least six

*Paydown Mill Stones. Photo by Loring Bullard.*

spring-powered mills each in the Meramec and Gasconade River Basins. Mills arrived later in the southern part of the state, but the North Fork Basin, heavily endowed with springs, eventually had at least five spring-powered mills; at places like Bryant, Hodgson, and Zanoni.

Some of the earliest spring-powered mills were sawmills, set amidst large expanses of virgin timber in east-central Missouri. In the *Old Settlers Gazette*, historian Lynn Morrow noted that by 1816 many sawmills were cutting shortleaf pine in the upper Gasconade and Big Piney watersheds. Much of this pine was sawed into planks and sent downriver to feed the St. Louis building boom. Water wheels at these mills operated large "sash saws," with vertically-mounted, six-foot blades.

For the miller, each individual spring site required a unique solution. Where there was enough head of fall, an elevated flume could be built, allowing the more efficient overshot water wheel to be used. Millers used locally available materials, when they could. Elm, which was rot resistant, was used to make water wheels and wheel paddles, and dense oak was used for shafts. Joseph Strain, who rode horseback from Tennessee to Pulaski County in 1840, built his mill of hand-hewn oak; its beams were held together with wooden pins; its foundation stones cut from limestone ledges along the nearby Gasconade River. It took him four years to build the mill.[3]

Millers imported their own lingo to describe complicated machinery. Most of the names for mill parts are now archaic—the "ether," the runner stone, the "nether," its lower mate, and the lignum, wallower, gudgeon, rynd, step cup, and horse. Adjusting the space between the stones was called "tentering," and "pecking tools" were used to sharpen and dress the stones.[4] Millstones made from Missouri stone were not hard enough to wear well (except for the volcanic rock rhyolite), so the best stones were imported, often from France, and were expensive, sometimes costing a year's wages for a skilled craftsman. Only rarely could the miller find the specialized tools he needed locally, so he usually brought them with him from elsewhere. Joseph Strain packed his millwright tools from Tennessee on a led horse.

Mill work was often uncomfortable and sometimes dangerous. Because flour dust was so explosive, no open flames were allowed in flour mills, so most weren't heated in winter. Belts and gears and spindles could snag clothes, pinch fingers, or much worse. Mills were usually operated by two men, at most, and as former miller Joe O'Neale explained, customers normally weren't invited into primary work areas: "They didn't allow just everybody and their dog up there."[5]

The miller extracted a fee for grinding, the toll, which was announced on a wall chart. According to O'Neale, often "there was no money changed hands." Workers weighed the customer's container of grain and gave them back "so much flour," and "kept so much." Many customers brought their grain in cloth bags and toted their own bags back home. "They'd wash those sacks and take care of them just like people now would take care of a pillow case," O'Neale recalled.

Equipment problems were frequent. Mats of watercress dislodged by muskrats or logs felled by beavers sometimes floated down raceways and lodged in the mill works. Human nature could also be at fault. "Kids like to throw rocks and watch them splash," O'Neale observed. "That current is so swift it'll carry a big rock right in there. That wears on the turbine right away." In his book *Ridge Runner*, Larry Dabblemont tells a story about a mill wheel that stopped turning in the middle of the night. Dabblemont's father, who worked at the mill, investigated, and to his horror, in the glare of his carbide light saw a person's white, dismembered leg caught in the waterwheel. He called the sheriff, who the next day reported that a twenty-pound eel had been found jammed into the works.

Customers often had to hang around the mill for hours or even days, waiting their turn. But this provided an opportunity to complete other errands, like getting horses shod, shopping at the general store, visiting with neighbors or participating in games. Boys winning foot races were said to be as "swift as a mill race." Nightly campfire revelry and fiddle music often kept the miller awake, and many a moonlight romance took place "down by the old mill stream." There was plenty of Dutch-oven cooking, with wafting scents of bacon and corn pone to accompany the "song of the maiden," the sound of grain rattling through the hopper. Mills frequently became centers of social life, sometimes hosting elections and church services in addition to meetings, picnics, and dances. Communities often congealed around mills, with blacksmith shops and general stores usually among the first businesses to be established.

*Falling Spring, Oregon County. Photo by Steve Spencer.*

Technological advances spelled the end of water mills, which had held their own since the days of the Romans. When steam power began replacing water-power, mills could be located anywhere. Most water-powered mills in Missouri were gone by the mid-1900s. Historian Paul Wobus, researching Missouri's mill sites, found that of 170 water-powered mills shown in the 1890 *Rand McNally Atlas*, almost all were out of business by the late 1920s.[6] By then, almost everyone bought their meal and flour at the grocery store.

Many old spring-supplied mills or mill dams, however, were eventually converted to small scale hydropower, providing electricity for local businesses, resorts, homesteads, or even towns. However, the variable nature of spring outputs could produce flickering electric lights or ones that dimmed as flows diminished. Electrical transmission distance could also be an issue. At Reed Spring, lights were bright at the mill/hydropower site but dim in the town of Centerville, a few miles from the mill.

For mill owners, being in personal control of the power source presented certain advantages. Former miller at Zanoni, Ralph Laughlin, remembered the old man who operated the mill's hydropower facility as "quite a genius." The man used hydropower to light up his home and

store. When he got ready to go to bed, he would go out and close the water gate, but the wheel would continue to turn for some time. "By the time he got ready and got into bed, the lights would finally go out."[7]

The state's second largest spring—Greer Spring—was once considered for a major hydropower facility. In 1905 Edward Shepard, a professor from Drury College in Springfield, was hired by St. Louis investors to determine the feasibility of building a dam below Greer Spring (then called Big Ozark Spring) to produce electricity. By this time, Missourians had become enthralled by the magic of electricity, which promised to enhance prosperity with labor-saving appliances and new jobs in milling, mining, and manufacturing. Engineers, speculators, and entrepreneurs were crawling all over Missouri's backwoods, searching for places to harness the power of flowing water.

Shepard found what he thought was a suitable dam site below the spring and in his report to potential investors, suggested that the electricity produced would find immediate application—powering local mines and lighting up distant cities like Springfield, St. Louis, and Memphis.[8] Obviously, the dam was never built. The

*Powerhouse at Maramec Spring. Photo by Loring Bullard.*

*Mill Spring, Wayne County. Photo by Steve Spencer.*

location may have been too remote, or the project possibly had been preempted by dams already being planned elsewhere, like the one on the White River at Powersite.

The old water mills are now mostly gone, but not entirely forgotten. In *Water Mills of the Missouri Ozarks*, George Suggs wrote that "the continuing influence of water mills on the American mind is less economic than artistic and aesthetic." This sense of the aesthetic values of springs and mills is deep-seated. When Luella Owens, a cave explorer and writer, visited Greer Spring in the 1890s, a bigger mill dam was being considered, to "turn to practical account the power now going so cheerily to waste." But if that were done, she noted with obvious lament, the "artistic loss would be proportionately severe."[9] Today, many if not most Missourians would agree with her.

Luckily, several mill structures still stand at Missouri springs—at Alley, Bennett, Boylers, Hazelton, Hodgson, Paydown, Rockbridge, Topaz, and Zanoni, for example. They evoke images of slower, simpler times, providing romantic backdrops or panoramic vistas along with a twinge of nostalgia. Such images still have great curb appeal. Hodgson Mill, for example, has been featured on the Missouri state highway map and the cover of the St. Louis phone directory.

Mills originally served utilitarian purposes, only later finding their ways into the hearts of Missourians as nostalgic and iconic structures. Today, old mills and their dams and ponds seem to fit comfortably into the native scenery. Some springs, however, were once centerpieces of major industrial enterprises far beyond the cutting of wood or grinding of grain. These operations were anything but scenic, but in their own ways advanced the interests of the state and its people. They provided the power to manufacture industrial materials and chemicals and even to help with the machinery of war.

## CHAPTER 6: FOUNTS OF INDUSTRY

IN HIS FIRST ANNUAL REPORT of the Geological Survey in 1855, Missouri's State Geologist, George Swallow, wrote that "iron stands pre-eminent in its influence upon the power and prosperity of a nation." At that time, it did. Iron drove the nation's great industrial expansion in the nineteenth century and Missouri iron played a significant role. In fact, Swallow forecasted that Missouri, with its extensive deposits of iron ore, would soon become the "great iron mart of the western continent."[1]

Earlier in the nineteenth century, Missouri-produced iron had not been available. Farmers needed plows and horseshoes and tradesmen needed machines and tools, but all of these had to be imported from eastern manufacturers, increasing prices by up to 100 percent. In 1821, at the time of Missouri's founding, the state had no iron works. For that reason, residents watched with interest and anticipation when Thomas James erected an iron furnace in central Missouri in 1829. James's choice of locations was dependent, in large measure, on the presence of a very large spring.[2]

James's father had been an iron monger, supplying cannon parts for the Continental Army in Virginia. Like his father, Thomas was a big man, standing six-foot eight. He would eventually follow in his father's footsteps in the iron business, but not before taking a detour. Moving west from Virginia in 1796, he invested in a salt-works in Ohio. The venture proved profitable, making James a wealthy man. But he apparently wanted more. He watched with interest as the charcoal iron industry advanced westward, reaching Kentucky and Tennessee by 1825.

According to a time-worn legend, James heard about a rich iron bank in Missouri from Shawnee Indians passing through Ohio on their way to visit the "Great Father" in Washington, D. C. As improbable as that story may be, James somehow also learned about a "great spring" near the iron deposits. It sounded too good to be true: rich iron deposits right at a gigantic spring, a never-failing source of power, surrounded by thousands of acres of trees for making charcoal.

James decided to risk his fortune on the new venture, acquiring over 10,000 acres around the spring for wood to fire his furnace and forges. He carefully assessed the iron deposits, which presented as "angry red scars" streaking the hillsides, much of it deposited in ancient sinkholes in the limestone. Near the deposits and the spring, he built a blast furnace, forges, and hammer mills. These complicated devices required a highly skilled labor force to operate and James and his partner, Samuel Massey, spent a small fortune transporting men and materials to Missouri from Ohio, six hundred miles away.

The spring was dammed and wooden sluices conveyed the stored water past four large undershot water wheels. These ran the sawmill, operated giant pistons that compressed air to blow into and super-heat the furnace, and turned grinding stones in the grist and flour mills. Spring power also turned cams to lift and drop the immense, spring-loaded refining hammers. Powerful blows from these 500-pound hammers literally beat the impurities out of the bars of raw iron poured and solidified from the furnace.

Thomas James must have been a pious man, or maybe simply practical, since an 1888 *Goodspeed History* stated there was "no saloon allowed" at the

*Maramec Spring. Photo by Steve Spencer.*

Maramec Works. Perhaps that was a key to its longevity. Thomas died in 1856 and his son, William, managed the business until 1878. For five decades, then, the James family provided good wages and full employment for many men. The James Family Foundation still owns the site, where the furnace survives, along with exhibits of the forges and refining hammer. The closest town is called St. James.

Another big spring in Missouri was at the center of iron production at a time when America was in dire need of the metal for war machines—the First World War. The military also needed high-powered explosives. World War I is sometimes called the "Chemists War," because for the first time in history the production of industrial chemicals largely determined how the war was fought, and won. This has little to do with springs, of course, but there is one place in Missouri where the proximity of a large spring to raw materials for chemical production led to the establishment of a major military-industrial complex—one intended to help our country win the war to end all wars.

I first read about the place in H. C. Beckman and N. S. Hinchey's 1944 book, *The Large Springs of Missouri*. The entry was "Midco Spring," located two miles north of Fremont, Missouri "at the site of the former town of Midco." That was enticing in itself, but the description continued: "In

*Refining Hammer, Maramec Iron Works. Photo by Loring Bullard.*

the past it was used for a water supply for the town of Midco and for the Mid-Continent Iron Company Plant, which has since been demolished."

I had never heard of this place, or else had forgotten about it (it is also mentioned in *Springs of Missouri*), and naturally I wanted to see it. Having already visited springs that had been used for powering mills, raising fish, filling swimming pools, supplying breweries and canneries, and for public and private water supplies, I thought this site might offer something different and unique—a ghost town, with a ghost plant, served by a ghost spring. How cool is that?

With topo map in hand, I visited the site of Midco for the first time on a foggy February morning. Arriving by 7 a.m., I parked at the end of the blacktop near a creek crossing. There was a driveway to the right but no houses nearby, so I quickly walked up the dry creek bed toward the spot I had marked on the topographic map—Midco Spring. Before long I saw rusted lengths of iron pipe in the stream bed and a hulking brick structure, resembling a bunker, on the left bank. To the right, in the weeds, were massive concrete foundations and partial walls and piles of bricks, and suddenly, as I stepped into a clearing, a very tall smokestack loomed over the misty, ghostly scene. It was eerie but amazing. I was standing in the rubble of Midco—a ghost town.

Further up the creek I found the spring itself, gushing from the foot of a seventy-foot, curved mural bluff, a clear lake at its base. Near the lake's edge, a circular rock and mortar spring basin squatted among the rocks, with several rusted iron pipes protruding from it—the water supply. I took pictures and hurried back to the car, but in April I visited the site again, this time talking to the landowners, who graciously offered to show me around. Later, Donna Sutton of the Carter County Library was kind enough to loan me a book about Midco.

In *Midco, Ghost Town of the Ozarks*, Mary Weaver wrote about visiting the site in 1913, before it became Midco. As she approached a bend in the valley north of Fremont, she saw a "gleaming, well-kept ranch house." In the kitchen "a continuous stream of water" flowed through the sink, and in the barnyard was a "huge, ever-flowing water trough," both served by the nearby spring. At the spring, Weaver noted a "perpendicular cliff with a yawning cave-like aperture, mirrored in the crystal waters."[3] Just a

*Midco Spring. Photo by Loring Bullard.*

few years later, that big spring and a huge tract of land surrounding it would play vital roles in the development of Midco.

The idea for Midco began with attempts to mine various minerals in southern Missouri in the 1890s. Much of the timber had already been cut by then in Carter, Ripley, and Shannon Counties, making the land more accessible and mineral extraction easier. In fact, it seemed like the next logical step. A small iron and manganese plant operated near the Current River north of Fremont, and prospects seemed promising there when a group of businessmen, mostly "young lawyers" from Kansas City, decided to form the Mid-Continent Iron Company—Midco.[4]

One of the partners, a wealthy Chicago businessman named George Peck, purchased 19,000 acres along Mill and Rogers Creeks, tributaries of the Current River. Here the partners figured they would find everything they needed for making iron—ore of a decent grade; water for workers and for manufacturing; and plenty of trees for charcoal to burn the ore. The company purchased a tract of land near the spring for the smelter and leased 3,700 acres of Peck's land for timber. Subsequently, the company added many more thousands of acres, some tracts as far as thirty miles away.

*Midco Smokestack. Photo by Steve Spencer.*

In the spring of 1917, work began on the smelter, which would've been in production a year later had the war not intervened. The U.S. Government noted the industrial potential at Midco and saw an opportunity to involve the facility in war efforts. In the words of one historian, the government "took complete charge—" not surprising, since the military was in dire need of iron for war machines and chemicals for explosives and manufacturing processes. Thus, the government became a "partner" in Midco, investing $1.5 million in the chemical manufacturing portion of the facility.

Largely, the federal government coveted the thick stands of timber in the vicinity, not the spring itself. Wood was a key ingredient for making acetone, a chemical necessary for the production of cordite, an explosive mixture of nitrocellulose and nitroglycerine. Acetone was also an important industrial solvent used to make the cellulose acetate "dope" to paint on airplane wings to stiffen and waterproof the canvas. Wood alcohol was used to denature ethyl alcohol (booze) to make it undrinkable but was also integral to a wide variety of military-industrial processes. Trees were the basic raw materials in all of these chemicals.

The feds paid for the construction of retorts, or ovens, where logs were heated without oxygen, giving off a thick vapor that condensed into a brownish liquid the workers called "wood vinegar." Lime, made from the locally abundant supply of limestone, was added to the vinegar solution to produce acetate of lime, or calcium acetate, an immediate precursor of acetone. A sawmill cut logs into lengths for the retorts or into chunks to make charcoal in the kilns. There was a power house, compressor house, repair shops, storage warehouses and shipping docks. A rail line run in from Fremont delivered ore, lime, wood, bricks, pumps, and parts. Some materials, such as wood, also arrived by wagons over recently improved roads.

Midco was in full production by the fall of 1918. Two-hundred tons of ore were unloaded daily, and the pile waiting to be smelted reached "gigantic proportions." The operation devoured trees voraciously. The charcoal-fired smelting furnace alone used 180 cords per day, or twelve acres of standing timber. At its peak, the plant employed at least 400 workers, providing an economic boost for a historically job-poor area. Scores of homes were built nearby, supplied with a post office, school, churches, a baseball field, and credit at the company store. Most of the homes and company buildings got their drinking water from the spring. The two-story, brick office building boasted "two fireplaces" and "running water from the spring."[5]

The town of Midco reportedly reached a population of nearly 3,000. Even adjacent landowners tried to get in on the action. An advertisement for "Fremont Heights," to be located one mile from Midco, screamed that it would soon become "the future city to house thousands." The ad offered 100 lots at "one-half the listed price." The would-be "city," however, never materialized.

Work at the plant was hot, dirty, and dangerous. Noel Bowen, age 16, was killed by a "falling furnace," and Charles Cominsey was severely injured after being "knocked from the top of a retort by a pair of pipe tongs." But what was more devastating to the labor force than accidents was the flu. When the worldwide pandemic of influenza, or Spanish flu, reached Carter County in October 1918, *Midco Notes* recorded morosely that the disease had been "doing its deadly work in the community. To date about twenty-five deaths are reported." Later that same month, construction work on the smelter plant came "almost at a standstill" because of the illness. On November 1, Mrs. Will Sanders died, the "seventh member of that family to succumb."

But even more powerful forces hurried the demise of Midco—the end of the war. Some of the neighbors were not altogether unhappy to see it go. One can imagine the pall of smoke that hung over the place, not to mention the dust, noise, and smell. Of course, there were few anti-pollution laws to worry about. In February 1921, Midco's general manager, Mr. Buseik, wrote a letter to officials

*Ruins at Midco. Photo by Loring Bullard.*

in the town of Doniphan, downstream on the Current River, explaining that the company had "discontinued the practice of dumping tar into the creek." And in a 1930 publication, Josiah Bridge claimed that chemical wastes from Midco flowing into nearby Davis Creek, a losing stream, had contaminated Big Spring, ten miles away.[6]

Shortly after the armistice, the federal government pulled out of Midco. Munition contracts were cancelled and the price of pig iron tumbled.[7] The owners decided to call it quits after producing almost 150 million tons of pig iron in only three years. A local paper in November 1921 noted that pursuant to an order of the court, the plant, said to be worth about $6.5 million, would be "sold on the blocks." A few prospective buyers showed interest, but the operation never re-booted. A parts liquidator from Pennsylvania bought much of the infrastructure for scrap. Bricks were cleaned and hauled off to Van Buren to build homes. What was left was left to itself, to be overgrown with weeds and re-taken by the surrounding forest.

The ruins of Midco stand in the weeds—mute sentinels to an almost-forgotten era. Midco Spring still flows, filling nothing but the nearby lake. The smokestack still rises from the ruins but provides few hints of the scale of enterprise once seen here. After WWI, the production of iron and chemicals moved to huge industrial complexes, where springs were no longer needed for drinking or cooling water or hydropower. Unfortunately, at the same time Missouri's burgeoning industries, both urban and agricultural—and the steam-roller of "progress" exemplified in widespread land grading, plowing, blasting, poisoning and dredging—spelled trouble for the state's waters, including its springs.

## CHAPTER 7: TROUT WATERS

FISHING WAS NOT SO HOT in Missouri in 1895 when the state's Fish Commissioner lambasted the "trammel-netters and dynamiters" for their extreme tactics and excessive takes.[1] Amazingly, both methods were legal at the time. Fish and game laws were weak to non-existent. Pollution of streams, removal of forests, and unenlightened farming practices had degraded streams and aquatic habitats. The state's stocks of fish had become severely depleted. In the eastern U.S., where even greater degradation had become evident, Izaak Walton adherents promoted fishing regulations and sustainable harvests.

Private fish and game propagation clubs sprang up in many places, including Missouri. Greene County's Club made "careful investigations of the temperature and purity" of local streams with a view toward restocking them with the "finest varieties of game and food fish."[2] But these efforts in no way constituted scientific fish management, and most of the re-stocking programs were dismal failures.

The federal government began to show an interest in helping out, largely in the person of Dr. Livingston Stone, a Unitarian minister with massive mutton-chop sideburns. Stone made a radical career change when he signed on as deputy of the newly established U.S. Fish Commission in 1872, working under Spencer Fullerton Baird, the nation's first Fish Commissioner and curator of the Smithsonian Institution. Baird instructed Stone to go to California, check out the salmon spawning grounds and build a hatchery. Railroad workers told Stone they had seen Indians spearing salmon by the hundreds in the McCloud River of northern California, so he directed construction of the first national fish hatchery there in 1872, now the world's largest hatchery complex. Within a few years, another hatchery, this one for rainbow trout, was built just upstream.[3]

Within a year of starting work for the Fish Commission, Stone was moving fish all over the country. On one such trip in the summer of 1873 he was transporting bass, catfish, and eels in a specially designed railroad car. Heading west from Omaha, he had just sat down for dinner and poured a cup of tea when he heard a tremendous crash. The car jolted and pitched steeply forward as the train plunged into a river. Stone found himself pinned under a heavy tank. As water rushed in, the tank lifted and Stone struggled free, only to be washed into the river. He managed to climb on top of the mostly submerged car. He was safe, but the fish were gone.

In spite of this mishap, Stone made many more trips. By 1882, the Commission had invested in improved fish cars, each able to carry 20,000 pounds of fish. Fish and humans alike traveled

*Brown Trout. Courtesy of Missouri Department of Conservation.*

first class in cars designed for safety and comfort. In the mid-1880s, Stone began looking for new hatchery sites closer to where fish were needed, and he set his eyes upon a place in Missouri. The state's legislators were supportive, knowing that a federal fish hatchery would elevate Missouri's status in the sport-fishing world.

Stone selected a place in Neosho, which had large springs to supply the hatchery. Water could flow by gravity directly to the fish-rearing ponds, eliminating pumping costs. Just as importantly, the site was served by a well-maintained railroad line, the primary avenue for hauling fish. The government purchased 17 acres near Hearrell Spring and completed construction of the hatchery there in 1889. The next year the first eggs arrived. The hatchery specialized in rainbow trout, but also raised crappie, bass, goldfish, channel cat, and bluegill.[4]

The hatchery worked hard to serve the public interest. In 1893 its fish were displayed at the World's Fair in Chicago. When Fort Crowder military base was established in 1941, the hatchery stocked Elm Creek, near the base, for the angling enjoyment of the soldiers stationed there. But in later years, federal budget cuts nearly eliminated the hatchery. Congressman Gene Taylor helped to rescue it as a "mitigation station," providing fish to replace the native bass that would be lost when the White River was impounded.

Before the end of the nineteenth century, the state of Missouri also got into fish propagation. All of the state's hatcheries were originally built at large springs. The first was at Brown Spring, near St. Joseph, probably because the chair of the Missouri Fish Commission lived there. Rainbow trout from the Brown Spring hatchery were stocked into Spring Creek, Crane Creek, and Blue Spring Branch. The Commission abandoned the hatchery in 1918 when the spring began to fail, probably because of increased development and groundwater pumping in the vicinity.

*Mark Van Patten Trout Fishing. Courtesy of Missouri Department of Conservation.*

In 1920, the Missouri Fish Commission purchased land for a hatchery at Sequiota Spring in Springfield. The hatchery and a few surrounding acres became Missouri's smallest state park. In 1958, the operation moved to the new Shepherd of the Hills Hatchery at the base of Table Rock Dam. Plenty of cold water could be drawn from the bottom of the reservoir (although it could be low in dissolved oxygen), so a spring was no longer necessary. The quality of water produced by Sequiota Spring had also declined over the years and this, too, may have been a factor in the move.

Today, Missouri has four sprawling, spring-based trout parks—Bennett Spring, Roaring River, Montauk, and Maramec Springs. Before it became a trout-fishing mecca, Bennett Spring was called Brice's Spring. Bennett, the later spring owner, sold the property to the state in 1925. Montauk became a state park in 1927, and a hatchery was constructed there shortly after WWII. At Roaring River Spring, a hatchery was built in 1912, but fifteen years later a flood destroyed the dam. A wealthy St. Louis businessman bought the property in 1928, turning it over to the state twenty-seven days later.

The ironworks at Maramec Spring operated until 1878. When William James died in 1912, he left the land to his great-granddaughter, Lucy James. Upon her death in 1938, the estate became part of the family trust. Lucy wanted the estate to remain in private hands but open for public enjoyment. The Missouri Department of Conservation took over operation of the hatchery and opened the Maramec Spring branch to trout fishing in 1943.

The involvement of the Conservation Department began an era of modern, scientific fisheries management. Two species of trout are raised in state hatcheries and stocked into Missouri streams—rainbows and browns. Rainbow trout are not native to Missouri, but as desirable game fish have been introduced into streams on every continent except Antarctica. They are native to cold water streams flowing into the Pacific Ocean from the coasts of Asia and North America. Missouri springs are about the perfect temperature for hatching and growing rainbows.

Missouri's other popular trout species, the brown, is native to Europe. These handsome black and orange speckled fish were originally introduced to North America from Scotland and Germany. In Missouri, the first brown trout fingerlings were released into streams near Neosho in 1892. By the 1920s, they were being widely stocked into Ozark streams. The higher expense of growing browns, however, and low takes compared to rainbows, led to a declining interest in them. Over time, attitudes changed. Stocking was reinstated in the 1950s, and in 1973 the first "trophy" brown trout status was obtained in the Meramec River.

Missouri springs work better for raising rainbows than for browns. Water temperatures much above 50 degrees F are not good for hatching brown trout eggs. The cold water coming out of the bottom of Table Rock Lake (40-50 degrees F), however, supplying the Shepherd of the Hills Hatchery, has proven ideal. These days, brown trout eggs are also "heat-shocked" for ten minutes in 83-degree F water. This produces a triploid fish, with 50% more chromosomes. Because these fish are sterile, they don't waste energy in spawning, allowing them to grow to larger sizes.[5]

I asked my fishing buddy, Skip Doak, about any problems from using springs to raise trout. Retired from the Missouri Department of Conservation, Doak is the former hatchery manager at Maramec Spring. Murky water, such as after a rain, didn't seem to bother the adult fish, he said, but low dissolved oxygen could be a problem, and high nitrogen levels could cause a serious disease called "pop-eye." Nitrogen compounds, which are soluble in water, are sometimes found at high levels in Missouri springs. Screens are used to aerate the water in an attempt to off-gas the nitrogen.[6]

Trout park hatcheries try to get fish to "fighting size" as soon as possible before releasing them into streams. In the early days, fish were fed a mixture of foods to attempt a well-balanced diet—clabbered milk, hard boiled eggs, chopped liver, wheat shorts. Lights were even put over raceways

*Crane Creek. Photo by Loring Bullard.*

to attract a natural food source—insects. All of this changed in 1959 with the introduction of "Purina Trout Chow," the beginning of standardized fish feed formulations.

Trout habitat in Missouri is limited to about 170 miles of spring-fed streams, less than one percent of the state's total stream miles. In a few of Missouri's spring-dominated creeks, rainbow trout that were stocked many decades ago have become self-sustaining populations. These "wild trout" live within one or two miles of spring sources in streams with stable, tree-lined banks, deep holes, and limited fishing pressure. Because of the constant year-round temperatures of spring branches, wild trout grow faster here than in northern streams, where the water is colder in winter.

Eight streams in the state now have naturally reproducing populations of rainbows. One of these unique, spring-fed streams is Crane Creek in southwest Missouri. Chris Vitello, retired Fisheries Division Chief with the Conservation Department, enjoys fly fishing in Crane Creek, calling it a "mystical place" for anglers. The creek contains the McCloud strain of red-band rainbow trout,

## CHAPTER 8: FISH FARMS

I N MISSOURI, COMMERCIAL FISH FARMS supply millions of fish for stocking, fee fishing, or even bait or pets. Most of these farms use springs as their water sources. At least forty springs in the state at one time or another were used commercially for growing fish. Ten of these springs are in the Meramec Basin alone, and five are in the Black River Basin. A table found in *Springs of Missouri*, published in 1974, listed fourteen springs in use at that time for privately-owned fish-rearing facilities. Today, only five of these remain in operation.

Ozark Fisheries, now owned by Larry Cleveland, was one of the state's earliest fish farms. Cleveland's grandfather and a partner began the business in 1926, at first growing trout in ponds supplied by six springs in the valley of Au Glaize Creek in Camden County. But the operation struggled—restaurants weren't willing to pay enough, Cleveland suggests. A friend, a buyer for Woolworths, recommended to Larry's grandfather that he consider raising goldfish, popular pets sold in "five and dime stores."[1]

Ozark Fisheries has been raising goldfish ever since, many of them of the fancy varieties—calico fans, shubunkins—along with koi. The operation now has 350 ponds, producing tens of millions of goldfish per year. I asked Cleveland if low water at the springs ever caused problems. "We're at the mercy of mother nature as much as any other farm," he replied, thoughtfully. They do have a fall back plan, though—re-circulating the spring water, if necessary. The fish are boxed up and shipped all over the country, mostly by FedEx and priority mail.

Randy Welpman's grandfather started raising ornamental goldfish in 1939 using a spring near Stover, Missouri. At one time the farm had about 600 ponds. Now it's down to 230—still a lot of work. I watched Randy, his son, and two helpers seining a pond, slogging through deep mud and dumping into five-gallon buckets the squirming shards that are golden shiners, the bait fish that has been the mainstay of the business since the early 1960s.

Welpman remembers his family's competition with the Japanese over fancy goldfish. The Asians had hundreds of years of selective breeding behind them, making it hard for Americans to compete. The Japanese even figured out a cheap way to get fish to America, designing a "little container," each holding one fish, and stacking them by the thousands in lieu of ballast water in the holds of ships returning to the U.S.[2]

At Westover Farms in Crawford County, I visited with Terry England and Lisa Schlueter. Lisa quit teaching 8th grade in Bourbon in 2006 and with her husband, Tom, took over management

CRYSTAL SPRINGS TROUT FARM, CASSVILLE, MO.

1A2239

*Crystal Springs Trout Farm. Courtesy of History Museum on the Square, Springfield.*

introduce outside pathogens into his stock. Marvin is proud of the fish farming business and its gains. "Aquaculture now supplies over fifty percent of the fish consumed in the world" he told me, smiling, although in the U.S., he claimed, "it is being regulated out of business."

There are definitely rules that must be followed. As with agricultural operations like cattle feedlots, animal wastes or chemicals from fish farms could impair the quality of nearby streams. Federal and state laws apply to these "concentrated aquatic animal production facilities." Cold water (trout) farms producing over 20,000 pounds of fish per year and warm water (e.g., minnows, goldfish, catfish) farms producing over 100,000 pounds per year must get state operating permits. Where water from the farm discharges to a stream, the permittee must monitor the outfall for water quality parameters such as suspended solids, ammonia, and biochemical oxygen demand (BOD—a measure of how much oxygen is consumed when organic matter, such as animal wastes, are broken down).[5] Of course, there are costs for all of this.

*McDade Spring, Former Fish Farm. Photo by Loring Bullard.*

I was surprised at the large number of defunct fish farms, and visited several of them—Wilkins Spring in Phelps County, McDade Springs in Crawford County, Crystal Spring in Barry County, and Ozark Trout Farm in Newton County—and wondered, what happened to them? Why did they close? When I asked these questions to some of Missouri's current fish farmers, the answers were similar: It's hard for small-scale fish operations to make a profit these days. There is also a widely held view that regulations have become more onerous, and compliance with them more expensive.

In spite of these concerns, a handful of fish farms still operate. There is plenty of demand for catchable fish, bait or pets. These fish are being turned out by the millions, and springs are still a big part of that picture. But springs have also been in demand for other leisure-time activities and recreational pursuits. A great many of the state's camps, resorts and lodges have been built around springs because their cool, clear waters have long been a natural magnet for play.

## CHAPTER 9: SPRINGS AT PLAY

ABOUT SIX MILES WEST OF SPRINGFIELD in a park-like setting lies the remains of a very large, concrete-lined pool, formerly the Clear Creek Swimming Pool. As a kid growing up in Springfield, I vaguely remember being there. My most vivid recollection is that the water was cold, but the slick, greenish bottom seemed even colder. It was a flow-through swimming pool, fed by a large spring tumbling from the foot of a bluff, nearby. The pool was constructed in about 1922 and, amazingly, remained in use until the 1970s. There were bathing beauty contests, swimming exhibitions, a trapeze with aerial artists, an in-the-water merry-go-round and lots of screaming kids for nearly half a century.[1] Now the basin is dry, the concrete crumbling.

Clear Creek was one of scores, maybe hundreds, of spring-fed swimming pools in Missouri in the nineteenth and twentieth centuries. Although these pools were scattered across the state, most of them were in the Ozarks, where clear, cold springs are common. The spring-fed Cool Brook Natatorium, five miles south of Rolla, opened in 1922 and became very popular, remaining in business until the 1960s. Missouri historian John Bradbury swam there as a kid. He also remembers the ornate rockwork around the swimming pool at Stoneydell, near Arlington, the "most notable local recreational spot on Route 66 for thirty years."[2]

Other pools are much older. Most of the pools constructed prior to the 1920s, however, were actually more about "bathing" and less about "swimming." These served mineral spring resorts, where patrons soaked in mineral-laden water in the hope that it would infuse into and heal their ailing bodies. In the 1880s, customers at the Blue Lick Resort in Saline County could bathe in two wooden, spring-fed pools, with circulation sufficient to keep the water "absolutely pure." At Sweet Springs bathers enjoyed two octagonal pools, each thirty feet in diameter, with cemented bottoms and sides. The mineral spring pool at McAllister Springs remained in use through the 1930s. By then, patrons could "find on hand at the office the newest styles of bathing suits." At Chouteau Springs the swimming pool survived until WWII, when the *Missouri WPA Guide* announced that swimming there cost twenty-five cents.[3]

By the 1940s, about the only place in Missouri to find a mineral water bathing or swimming pool was at Excelsior Springs. The famous Hall of Waters in Excelsior, a gleaming art deco building constructed in the late 1930s using WPA funds, contained a glazed tile, 110,000-gallon, 84-degree heated pool filled from a sulpho-saline spring along the nearby Fishing River. A smaller "polio pool," complete with a wheelchair ramp, allowed patrons to take the cure pioneered by FDR at

Warm Springs, Georgia. Over time, pools became larger and more sanitary, catering to recreational swimmers and serving increasingly urban populations. In Springfield, several of the city's municipal swimming pools were once fed by springs. When built in 1915, Grant Beach pool was one of the largest in the Midwest, featuring a spring entering the pool through an imported sand "beach." The

*Mineral Water Pool at Excelsior Springs. Author collection.*

pool at Fassnight Park was supplied by a spring cascading over an attractive rock fountain. Several spring-fed swimming pools in the St. Louis area remained open until fairly recently. Almost all of them are now gone, after the properties became more valuable for subdivisions or commercial or industrial development.[4]

In addition to supplying pools, springs added to the atmosphere and allure of hotels and restaurants. Big Spring in downtown Neosho, self-proclaimed "city of springs," gushes into a nicely manicured park. It once provided drinking water for the city. Just below the spring stood the Big Spring Inn, a rambling hotel and restaurant featuring a spring-filled pool where patrons could catch their own dinners. Guests got a one-trout meal for ninety cents or two for a dollar. The Big Spring Inn attracted many famous personalities, such as Harry and Bess Truman, before it burned in 1966.[5]

Springs and spring-fed pools were popular attractions at a large number of Scout camps, YMCA camps, religious camps and resorts. Keener Springs Resort, managed by Lee and Robin Cotrell, is on the banks of the Black River. When I visited on an overcast day, the Black River lived up to its name, appearing dark and somewhat foreboding. The spring boils up in a short, curiously angular sandstone canyon before joining the river. A mill once stood near the spring, and during repair work a few years ago contractors excavated the large wooden axle of a mill wheel. Just uphill from the spring is the wide, arched opening of Keener Cave. The Cotrells once launched their canoe on the

*Big Spring Inn, Note Card. Author Collection.*

lake inside the cave. "It doesn't go back all that far," Robin laughed. When the resort hosts weddings, she hangs a chandelier inside a wooden arbor just outside the cave entrance.[6]

Stone Mill Spring on the Big Piney River supplied a clubhouse, now long gone, for officers at Ft. Leonard Wood. Brook Spring provided water for a Boys and Girls Camp in Phelps County, although the spring was abandoned in 1955 after it "turned dark."[7] St. Louis Masons relaxed at the Alhambra Grotto west of Newburg. The "grotto" was actually a rock enclosure built to protect the spring. A spring served Camp Beaver in McDonald County, but the little cabins there have now been converted to apartments. In fact, many of the camps and lodges once served by springs are either completely gone, falling into ruin, or have been repurposed.

I was eager to visit some of the old resorts that were built at springs. Two of them—Nagogami Lodge and Pippin Place—were on the Gasconade River in central Missouri. Both of them were once bustling places, attracting clientele from near and far. In an article for the *Old Settlers Gazette*, John Bradbury described how these resorts, once prominent high points on the social landscape, came to be so popular—and why they eventually faded.

After World War I, there were dozens of resorts and lodges on the Gasconade River catering to fishermen, hunters, and tourists. Many people came to escape the summer heat of the big cities. The Frisco Railroad, which intersected or paralleled the Gasconade River at several places between St. Louis and Springfield, delivered patrons quickly, efficiently, and cheaply to these destinations, and advertised the resorts extensively.

The Nagogami Lodge originally catered mostly to sportsmen stepping off of trains in Arlington, Dixon, and Jerome. In its later years, with better access to highways, Nagogami served mostly automobile travelers. I approached the old lodge on a sunny, pleasant December day, slowly cruising state blacktop road E, which ends near Gaines Ford on the Gasconade River. Having already visited many "forgotten" sites in Missouri, I wasn't all that surprised to find that

NAGOGAMI LODGE
ROLLA, MISSOURI

*Nagogami Lodge. Courtesy of the John Bradbury Collection.*

Nagogami, too, had that "end of the road" feel—abandoned buildings, crumbling rock walls, cracked and heaving concrete paths and stairways. On the hillside squatted the large concrete tank that might have once contained the spring water supply.

Before Nagogami became a resort, Boy Scout troops from Rolla used it as a campsite. The two-story lodge, built in 1923, had guest rooms above a large kitchen and dining room on the ground floor. Patrons could also stay in one of the modest cottages or in the smaller, more rustic cabins. The widely advertised specialty was fried chicken. The remote location offered solitude and relaxation, but that also meant few nearby services. Regardless, the rooms were frequently filled, even during the height of the Depression in the 1930s. The resort finally closed its doors for good in 1955.[8] When I visited in 2018, I parked near the river. I thought about asking a resident of one of the remaining cabins if I could have a look around, but thought better of it. Instead, I turned around and headed for Pippin Place, over sixty miles upstream on the Gasconade.

Pippin Place at Bartlett Spring was the brainchild of Dr. Bland Pippin, born and raised nearby. He originally purchased the large tract of land to "find solitude among the rugged hills" and "gurgling springs." As a kid, Pippin shelled corn and took it to Bartlett Mill, powered by the impounded water of Bartlett Spring. He eagerly anticipated these runs to the mill because while the miller was working, he had ample opportunities to fish or swim in the river. In 1911, Pippin

*Stoneydell. Courtesy of the John Bradbury Collection.*

bought forty acres near the spring and three years later began working on the resort. He hired men who couldn't pass their military physicals and put them to work felling giant oaks for dimension lumber, hauling sand and gravel from the river, or driving loads of cement from the railhead.[9]

Pippin tore down the three-story mill and replaced it with a two-story lodge. A five-kilowatt generator provided electricity via the turbine Pippin had salvaged from the mill—the first electricity ever seen in Pulaski County. The brightness of lights at the lodge depended on how much water passed through the turbine. Many times, patrons noted that lights were as dim as "coal oil lamps," but storing water behind the dam during the day provided more energy for the night.[10]

It was Dr. Pippin's son, Dru, who eventually took over and became general manager and whose name became associated with the resort for most of its existence. Dru Pippin was an avid conservationist, serving on Missouri's Conservation Commission for seventeen years. He wrote "Story of a River: An Autobiography of the Gasconade" for the October 1948 *Conservationist*.

"He knows the Ozarks, their hills, streams, and springs, and is an expert fly-fisherman, swimmer and canoeist," a promotional flyer enthused.

Frisco flyers heaped on the praise for Pippin Place, attracting clientele and pushing tickets to get there. Promoters noted the healthy nature of the "principal spring," which "flows up through a clean gravel bed." Further, the proprietors went out of their way to protect it: "Due precautions are taken in sanitation of the premises to prevent contamination of the water supply, which is unexceled for purity." An electric pump forced the spring water into a concrete storage tank sixty feet uphill from the lodge. This elevation, plus the force of gravity, provided "ample pressure" for indoor facilities.

A dam across the spring branch formed a "beautiful lake of clear spring water" providing "safe boating for children." In the nearby river, the spring produced an "invigorating temperature for swimmers." The seventeen-room cobblestone and concrete hotel featured "big wooden beams on high ceilings," a "massive fireplace where a cheerful fire warmed guests on frosty fall mornings and evenings," and "a huge bell, which summons guests to family-style meals." Although not fireproof, the structure was afforded "excellent protection by the water system."

The food was marvelous, of course. The owners were fortunate to have the same cook for forty-three years, a man whom Duncan Hines called "John, Dean of Chefs," famous for his "cooking, his love of people, and his loyalty to the Pippin family." His reputation for excellent "hot rolls, cornbread sticks and peppermint ice cream" spread far and wide. His biscuits were said to be "as light as the leaves drifting down the Roubidoux," delicious when dribbled with "honey as golden as the fall colors."

But like most resorts of the era, Pippin Place declined in usage after WWII and finally closed its doors in 1969. The main structure burned in 1984. The property is now owned by Jimmy Laughlin, who graciously let me in for a look around. Because of trespass and vandalism problems, Laughlin has installed a locked gate at the property entrance. From there, it is still over two miles on a dirt track back to the spring and lodge site. Even in ruin, the lodge is impressive. The standing rock walls remain tall, straight, and true, suggesting the quality of workmanship and former magnificence of the place. Nearby Bartlett Spring still wells up bright and blue before spilling over a concrete dam, part of the old hydropower system. Laughlin talks about the possibility of restoring the old lodge, although he knows it would be difficult.

Bradbury attributes the demise of Pippin and other resorts at least partly to the rise of the automobile. Better roads and multiple choices for lodging experiences greatly expanded

*Remains of Clear Creek Swimming Pool. Photo by Loring Bullard.*

opportunities for tourists and travelers. The inconvenience of resorts off the "beaten track" no doubt deterred some people, and many travelers were looking for diversions more exciting than the traditional pursuits of fishing, swimming in the river, or relaxing in a cottage, enjoying a glass of sparkling cold spring water.

Over the decades, springs fell out of favor as amenities necessary for the operation of resorts or swimming pools or camps. But it was not because Missourians had lost interest in outdoor recreation. In fact, over time, more and more people would head to the state's springs and spring-fed rivers and streams for a variety of recreational activities. But in the early part of the twentieth century, more and more people worried that, at some point, these beautiful places might not be available or accessible to a public becoming ever hungrier for what they had to offer.

## CHAPTER 10: SPRING PARKS

MISSOURIANS HAVE LONG USED AND ADMIRED their rivers, streams, and springs, but until the twentieth century gave little thought to preserving or protecting them. Water pollution only hit the national radar in 1899, and peripherally, at that, with passage of the Rivers and Harbors Act. This legislation made it illegal, for the first time, to dump garbage and refuse into the nation's waterways. Remarkably, in light of today's extensive water pollution laws, the Act was intended primarily to keep waterways free of debris for navigation purposes.

Missouri had very few water-pollution laws prior to World War II. Land and water protection before then most often involved setting aside outstanding land as parks, and lands with springs were some of the most outstanding the state had. One of the first springs in Missouri to be mentioned as a state park candidate was Ha Ha Tonka in Camden County. Governor Herbert Hadley suggested it in 1909, and a committee of the state legislature recommended it in 1915. But it wasn't to be—not yet.

A legend claims that Ha Ha Tonka means "smiling waters," but ethnographers have suggested the Indian words more nearly match "big laugh," which makes more sense. This beautiful spring, which flows into the Niangua River (now, Lake of the Ozarks), once powered a grist mill and a small community grew up around it. The surrounding area is probably the state's most striking example of karst topography, with a large natural bridge and many caves and sinkholes pocking the landscape.

In 1903, wealthy Kansas City businessman Robert Snyder visited Ha Ha Tonka Spring while on a hunting trip. He fell in love with the area, eventually buying 5,000 acres around the spring. In 1905 he began building his "dream castle" on the dolomite bluff overlooking the spring. Adrian van Brunt of Kansas City designed the castle, and to stimulate authenticity, Snyder brought in stone masons from Scotland. A tiny railroad was constructed to bring sandstone blocks from a nearby quarry.[1]

Snyder never completed his mansion. He was killed in an auto accident the next year. His sons finished it, although not to their father's exacting standards. A few years later they tried selling their amazing property to the state for a park, but funds sufficient for the purchase were not available. Not surprisingly, given the magnificence of Ha Ha Tonka, the family began making plans for a resort there in the 1920s. But that idea hit a snag when Union Electric began planning a dam on the Osage River—a dam that would back warm water over the cold, trout-filled pond below

*Roaring River Spring. Photo by Steve Spencer.*

fourth largest, providing two miles of trout fishing water on its way to join the Niangua River.

Within a few years of the first round of purchases, five more parks were added, three of them at springs—Montauk, Chesapeake, and Roaring River. Montauk Spring, acquired in 1926, was before 1892 a single-outlet spring welling up into the headwaters of the Current River. Then a big flood came through, filling the spring outlet with sand and gravel. The clogged spring reportedly "belched for several days" before breaking out at multiple, smaller outlets.

Roaring River arises from Roaring River Spring, so called because in the days before a dam was built at the outlet, the water cascaded loudly over broken ledges and boulders. On the opening day of trout season, March 1, I sat at a picnic table on the banks of Roaring River with Bill Bryan, the early spring sunshine warming our backs. Tall and red-haired with a boyish grin, Bryan is the former Director of Missouri State Parks.

Our meeting at Roaring River was appropriate—not only because Bryan is an ardent fly fisherman, but also because his father once served in the CCC here. Bryan cast glances at fishermen and -women working the river nearby as he reminisced about his father—how, near the end of his life, he still wanted to "go see the springs," one of his favorite outings. Bryan then reflected on the character of the individual parks. "Each trout park has its own unique personality," he suggested. Bennett Spring caters to the "hardened trout fisherman—people who are there to rip lips." Montauk is different, "more of a social scene—bonfires, coffee tents; the crowds are much different." Roaring River, too, has a unique personality, and history.[2]

Bryan told me about Thomas Saymen, the wealthy St. Louis "soap salesman" who bought the Roaring River property in 1928. The previous owner had built a hatchery at the spring, but in 1927 a flash flood destroyed the dam. 100,000 trout were washed into Roaring River, bankrupting the owner. Saymen bought the property "on the courthouse steps" and made plans to improve the facilities and stock the river with trout. But instead, he held onto the property only briefly before donating it to the state. Most likely, when he thought about how far Roaring River was from St. Louis or other big cities, he began to doubt that he could ever make the venture profitable.

Today, Roaring River caters to fishermen, campers, and tourists as a state-owned and operated facility. Profitability is not as much an issue. However, the park is an important economic driver for the region. Bryan points out that Cassville, the nearest city to the park, benefits greatly, servicing visitors with restaurants, motels, and other park-related businesses. He quoted a study, now somewhat dated, which indicated that for every dollar Missourians invest in their state parks, the economy sees twenty-six dollars of value.

I asked Bryan what Parks was doing to protect their central asset at this park, Roaring River Spring. The Department, he said, has been working to delineate the recharge area of its springs, since most of those areas lie outside of park boundaries. They have also concentrated on "reducing the risks by controlling upgradient land as much as possible." For instance, the Park Board purchased resorts just upstream of Bennett Spring in order to get rid of aging, failing septic systems. Most people don't realize it, Bryan said, but "ten miles upgradient of Bennett Spring is still in the park." "Significant" amounts of land have also been purchased in the recharge areas of Roaring River and Montauk Spring.

The Parks Division, Bryan suggests, has also exerted a considerable effort toward educating the public about springs and karst topography, teaching people about the "connections between the land and the beautiful springs." Bryan is proud of what has been accomplished at the trout parks, and that public agencies have worked so well together. "The Conservation Department grows and stocks the fish. DNR protects the resources and runs the parks. This is one of the longest standing, best partnerships in state government."

Bryan's father was one of the men who built the iconic structures that now grace Roaring River and other state parks, where the legacy of the CCC is prominently displayed. Two days after his inauguration in 1933, FDR got the Civilian Conservation Corps rolling through the Emergency Conservation Act, in part to "provide for the restoration of the country's depleted natural resources." The Army ran the CCC camps

*Bennett Spring Postcard. Courtesy of Missouri State Historical Society.*

and the Agriculture Department (through its Forest Service) and Interior Department (through the National Park Service) were responsible for work projects and management. Professional architects, foresters, engineers, and stone masons supervised the work.[3]

Near the main CCC office in St. Louis, notices were posted in shop windows and on billboards. Acceptance letters usually brought shouts of joy as young men who were nearly destitute suddenly became breadwinners, able to bring home $30 a month. Within a year, the National Park Service had established CCC work camps at Alley Spring and Big Spring State Parks. A year later, there were over 4,000 CCC workers in twenty-two camps at fifteen of the state's parks. By the end of 1936, over twenty-five million dollars of New Deal money had been spent in Missouri, much of it in the parks.

The CCC built roads, trails, bath houses and stately lodges. They built stone dams and spillways at Bennett Spring, Montauk, and Roaring River. They built outstanding bridges—the one at Bennett Spring with the three "Cs" of the CCC represented by the graceful arches has been called "the most perfect masonry-work the CCC ever produced." At Big Spring, workers fitted a pump in the spring to provide the camp and public campground with water. They built rustic stone cabins and a handsome dining lodge.

*View under Bennett Spring Bridge. Photo by Steve Spencer.*

Thanks to the state and the CCC, springs in state parks are now better protected. But there are hundreds of springs out there with little or no protection, many of them sustaining the flows of our state's most scenic streams. Obviously, springs and streams are intimately connected. One cannot protect the springs and forget the rivers, or vice versa. They have to be protected together, if at all. As Andy Ostmeyer, a writer for the *Joplin Globe*, puts it, we need to see our region "not as a collection of isolated springs and independent rivers, but as one interconnected and interdependent geologic organism."[4] There is no doubt that Missouri's most scenic rivers and their connected springs are part of one very beautiful and fluid entity.

## CHAPTER 11: SCENIC RIVERS, CROWN JEWELS

SPRINGS ARE CRITICAL TO THE QUALITY and flow of many of Missouri's finest streams. No one understood this better than Oscar "Oz" Hawksley. With his square black glasses and silver hair combed back, Oz looked the part of the absent-minded professor, and for many years he did teach biology classes at Central Missouri State College (now University of Central Missouri). Growing up in upper New York State, Hawksley built wooden boats and hiked and camped in the Adirondack wilderness. He developed a love of whitewater boating and worked for commercial river rafting companies in Utah and Arizona. In 1960, he ran Idaho's exciting Selway River in a Grumman aluminum canoe.

Hawksley began canoeing Missouri streams with friends in the 1950s. He is best remembered in this state for his float guide, *Missouri Ozark Waterways*, which has probably resided in more ammo cans or watertight boxes than any other book. In the 1950s, dams were the major threats to both rivers and their springs. As Hawksley remembered it, "it seemed like every river in Missouri was destined for a dam." In fact, a glance at Corps of Engineers maps of the time largely verified this. On a canoe trip on the Buffalo River in Arkansas, sitting around a campfire, Hawksley suggested that he and his friends start a floating club to "get people out on streams; to show them our streams have great recreational value."[1]

They soon formed the Ozark Wilderness Waterways Club. A sports writer for the *Kansas City Star*, Ray Heddy, "gave the club great publicity." The club got involved in saving the Meramec from a proposed dam, and with Harold and Margaret Hedges and Dr. Neil Compton in Arkansas, formed the Ozark Society, primarily to fight a dam planned for the Buffalo River. Members of both organizations worked together, even taking a bus to Washington D.C. to give testimony before Congress.

This, and a lot of grassroots organizing from many other quarters, stopped some of the most bitterly contested dams. A few of the best free-flowing rivers and their marvelous springs were saved, for the time being, but they were not exactly safe from all threats. After all, the watersheds of the rivers, as well as the recharge areas of their connected springs, were not entirely protected. The idea, though—that these resources had real value just as they were—had caught on.

Many of the same people who fought the dams later turned their attention to some kind of permanent protection for the state's most scenic rivers. Proponents of free-flowing rivers had already identified three rivers in Missouri with outstanding values—excellent water quality,

*Trout Fishing on Eleven Point River. Photo by Loring Bullard.*

*Upper Outlet, Big Spring. Photo by Gayle Harper.*

beautiful scenery, and relatively undisturbed watersheds—the Current, Jacks Fork, and Eleven Point. Feeding these rivers are some of the state's largest and most picturesque springs—what Jerry Vineyard referred to admiringly as Missouri's "crown jewels."

Congress passed a bill protecting the Current and Jacks Fork in 1964, the first federally protected streams in the nation. The legislation creating this park, the Ozark National Scenic Riverways (ONSR), provided for the protection of "free flowing streams," but also the "preservation of springs and caves." At least the outlets, if not the entire recharge areas of springs in the ONSR are protected. There can be no uses in the springs or spring branches that might impair their quality—such as removing plants (including watercress), disturbing the stream bottom, and in most of them, swimming or wading.[2]

The ONSR legislation also spelled out that Big Spring, "certainly by virtue of its magnitude alone," could well be the most "valuable single resource feature in the park." Therefore, any

*Blue Spring on Eleven Point River. Photo by Loring Bullard.*

activities that might affect it "must be judged using the highest standards." That may be why, at the dedication of the ONSR in June 1972, Tricia Nixon Cox, daughter of the president, christened the park by tossing a bouquet of flowers into Big Spring.

The legislation creating the Ozark National Scenic Riverways would serve as a model for the National Wild and Scenic Rivers Act passed a few years later, in 1968. Among the first group of rivers in the nation protected under the Wild and Scenic designation was Missouri's Eleven Point River, administered by the U.S. Forest Service. The Eleven Point watershed contains some of the state's largest and most beautiful springs. Greer Spring, Missouri's second largest, nearly doubles the flow of the Eleven Point River. Its spring "branch" is really a river in itself, although Forest Service rules preclude any "wading, swimming, boating, or floating" there.

Many miles downstream on the Eleven Point, near the end of the designated scenic section, Blue Spring, the state's twelfth largest, and Morgan Spring, at the site of the old Thommason Mill, enter the river at "The Narrows." Taking the walking path along the high, narrow ridge provides an outstanding view of Blue Spring, the river, and its deep confluence with Frederick Creek. A little

*Dam and Old Turbine at Boze Mill Spring. Photo by Steve Spencer.*

further upstream on the Eleven Point are Turners Mill Spring, where a metal mill wheel over thirty feet in diameter stands vertically in the spring branch, and Boze Mill Spring, impounded behind a mossy rock dam, where a rusting turbine lies in the channel.

The ONSR and Eleven Point Wild and Scenic River contain a treasure trove of magnificent springs, including Big, the biggest, and Blue, the bluest. But there are many others—Alley Spring on the Jacks Fork, for example, and Welch Spring on the Current, once the site of a sanitorium for asthma sufferers. Many of Missouri's other scenic rivers are also sustained by springs. Springs feeding the North Fork River, a popular floating and fishing stream, include Rainbow Spring, site of a former trout farm, Topaz Spring, with its restored grist mill, and Althea Spring, which once powered a small hydroelectric plant.

Boiling Spring, Miller Spring, and Shanghai Spring augment the flow of the Big Piney River, and Schlicht Mill Spring, Bartlett Mill Spring, Falling Spring, and another Boiling Spring add

*Blue Spring, Eleven Point River.*
*Photo by Loring Bullard.*

considerable flow to the Gasconade. Scenic Reed Spring, with its reconstructed mill, flows into the nearby Black River, while Howes Mill Spring enters the Huzzah. The spring issuing from Onondaga Cave feeds into the Meramec, and Bryant Creek receives flow from the beautiful springs at Hodgson Mill and Rockbridge. Bennett Spring, one of the most visited springs in the state, and Ha Ha Tonka Spring, at the bottom of a scenic gorge, add voluminous flow to the Niangua.

Many of the springs along these major streams issue from caves, which certainly invite exploration. But we have to be more careful these days. Cave ecosystems are fragile, as are the spring waters trickling across their floors. People have accidentally introduced pathogens, such as the one causing white-nose syndrome, into bat populations in caves. Cavefish populations have been reduced by collectors and cave disturbance. But scientific explorations of caves and springs have added to our knowledge of these fascinating natural features, and will aid us in our efforts to better protect them from harm in the future. Not surprisingly, the urge to explore them has a long and colorful history.

## CHAPTER 12: EXPLORING MISSOURI SPRINGS

LUELLA OWENS HAD AN OVERWHELMING URGE to explore caves, and to write about her caving adventures. She was an early geologic tourist, science writer, and spelunker. Slender and pretty, she grew up in St. Joseph, graduating from high school there in 1872. Further educated in the East, she traveled widely, making a trip around the world. While researching for her book on caves, she visited many sites in the Ozarks, including some of its largest springs.

In the 1890s, Owens visited Mammoth Spring in Arkansas, just over the state line. On the same trip, she explored the nearby chasm in Missouri known to locals as the "Grand Gulf." This eerie, steep-sided gash in the earth, nine miles northwest of Mammoth Spring, is part of a cave system that collapsed long ago. Dye tracing has confirmed that surface water entering this sinkhole comes out at Mammoth Spring. Owens heard there was a cave at the bottom, and she was determined to check it out.

With two assistants, she scrambled down the steep slope into Grand Gulf. They entered the cave at one end of the chasm, lit candles, and "sat down to wait for our eyes to adjust themselves." Less than a hundred feet into the cave, the explorers came to the end of dry land at a "silently flowing river." To Owens' surprise there was a boat there, tied with twine to a log, which her guide showed "no eagerness to appropriate to his own use." Around the boat, swimming close to shore, they saw "numerous small, eyeless fish, pure white and perfectly fearless—the first I had seen, and little beauties."[1]

The intrepid Owens got into the boat alone and leaving the twine attached, pushed off, drifting with "surprising speed," guiding the boat with her hands around curves in the six-foot wide channel. After several turns the journey ended abruptly when the ceiling lowered to a foot above the water's surface. She held her candle aloft, looking around, then lowered it to the water surface where she again saw the little white fish. They swam near the boat in an "astonishing multitude," as "unconscious of any possible danger as bees in a flower garden." Even dipping her hand into the water "occasioned no alarm, and they might have been caught by the dozens."

Suddenly her guide called out from behind that he feared the sharp rocks might cut the twine, leaving her no way to get back. Her exploration was "indefinitely suspended" and she was hauled back. She later wrote about the experience in her book about caves of the Ozark region (and Black Hills), a narrative that would intrigue explorers and scientists alike, and that nearly a century later would provoke an unusual subterranean investigation.

*Mammoth Spring Hydropower Dam. Photo by Steve Spencer.*

In 1984, St. Louis conservationist Leo Drey bought Grand Gulf and 322 acres of surrounding land and donated it to Missouri for a state park, to be operated under a lease agreement with his foundation. Grand Gulf had already been designated a National Natural Landmark in 1971. Park officials naturally wanted to know more about what they had acquired. They knew Luella Owens' story—about the cave, the boat, the cavefish. But none of that was accessible now. Local historians claimed that the great cyclone of 1921 had flushed logs and debris into the Gulf, plugging up the cave. Water had backed over the cave opening, and there was now a murky pond there. But what lay below its surface? How could park officials get a look at what Owens had seen? Were there still cavefish down there?

*Grand Gulf Holding Water. Photo by Steve Spencer.*

Their attempt to unravel the mystery involved hiring a consulting firm, which sent one of its engineers, Tim Smith, to investigate. I sat down with Smith at a restaurant in Springfield, where he told me the ups and downs of his journey of exploration with Grand Gulf. The presumption of park officials, Smith said, was that wood and debris had plugged the small passage leading to the underground river. If that plug could be removed, then the river might be explored. Unfortunately, the discovery process would be nowhere near that simple.

In the fall of 1985, a first group of engineers had tried to pump out the water sitting over the plugged passage, two hundred vertical feet below the rim of the sinkhole. It was a dismal failure. First, they used the wrong kind of pipe, and then, as soon as the system was reconfigured and the pump re-started, the pipe blew apart. DNR officials called in Smith at that point to get the project "across the finish line." He re-engineered the piping system, but to no avail. "On the same

*The Gulf, A Big Sinkhole in Oregon County.*
*Photo by Steve Spencer.*

day," he said, laughing, "we burned up the pump, we ran out of money, and we ran out of time."[2]

In the spring of 1988 Joe Goedde, an engineer with State Parks, asked Smith to come back, saying he really wanted to "see what's down there." They contracted with a diver, Gary Rummel, who first tried to go in with regular scuba gear. But as soon as he entered the "puddle" it turned to mud. He couldn't see a thing, although he "felt around as much as he could." They next sent him back in a diving helmet with a built-in communication line. He still couldn't find the entrance of the passage and once after a long, quiet period, Smith heard him say, "I'm stuck." Smith's blood pressure shot up. Rummel got free, but the plan was abandoned.

The project leaders next contacted David Summers, head of the Hydraulic Mining Institute at UMR (now MST) in Rolla. Summers was an avid tinkerer as well as an acronym-lover, and he built a robotic underwater camera, dubbing it the Submersible Television Exploratory Vehicle, or STEVE. The mini-vehicle was ready in 1991 and was sent in. While folks on the surface watched on a screen, STEVE made it back to a point where the passage necked down to 15 to 20 feet wide. But it was only a foot high—and STEVE was a foot tall—so that was the end of the line for him.

STEVE did glimpse something of the passage ahead, with no obvious blockages. Summers had another brainstorm. "Why don't I invent a robotic underwater excavator?" In the summer of 1992, ROWER (Remotely Operated Water Excavation Robot), a tracked vehicle using water jets for cutting power, was ready to deploy. But right then hurricane Andrew hit, and inland storms sluiced large quantities of mud and gravel into the cave mouth. A clam-shell digger was brought in to remove it, but two or three more storms in quick succession brought in a lot more debris, making the effort appear hopeless.

At that point Smith suggested another tactic. Why not drill a borehole from the surface into the cave conduit below, where camera equipment could be inserted for a look around? Of course, sophisticated geophysical equipment would be needed to accurately locate the spot on the land surface directly above the cavern below, and that would be fairly expensive. Geologists at DNR scoffed, suggesting that it would never work. So that idea was abandoned, too. Besides, the state had run out of money. The whole project was canned. The

*Inside Devils Well. Photo Courtesy of Jo Schaper.*

secret passageway described by Luella Owens may never be seen again. But then again, it might.

Other underground openings are still accessible, at least to expert explorers. One of these exciting cave/spring complexes lies in the Ozark National Scenic Riverways. Canoeists on the Current River can paddle right into the outlet of Cave Spring, welling up under an impressive bluff. What can't be seen from the river is the extensive cave and underground lake inside the bluff. In 1956, Jerry Vineyard discovered a "secret" passage into this subterranean labyrinth called Wallace Well, a pit in a small cave just downstream of the Cave Spring outlet. The pit opened downward into an underground lake sixty feet long, thirty feet wide, and 150 feet deep.

This lake, in turn, was found to be connected to Devils Well, a karst feature on the uplands further from Cave Spring.[3] Visitors arrive at this sinkhole/natural well via a county road, traveling downhill for a considerable distance before reaching the bottom of a valley. Although the elevation here is much lower than the ridgetop above, visitors are actually nowhere near the "bottom." For when they exit the parking lot and take the stairs down to the "bottom" of the sinkhole nearby, they can peer even further downward, into a "bottomless pit." A motion-sensitive light comes on

*Looking down into Devils Well. Photo by Loring Bullard.*

so they can see the surface of the lake, far below. It's almost enough to induce vertigo.

The property owner, at one time, installed a hand-powered winch here, attached to a bosun's chair, a device originally designed to transfer people from boat to boat on a suspended cable. Jerry Vineyard descended in the chair in 1956 for preliminary mapping of the chamber, which turned out to be gigantic—400 feet long, 100 feet wide and 300 feet in vertical extent. At the bottom, the chamber bells out. It contains one of the largest known underground lakes in the country, more than 400 feet long and over 200 feet deep. Geologists lowered a boat and paddled on the lake, taking its measurements and marveling at the numerous waterfalls adding to its volume. This has to be one of the most stupendous spring plumbing systems ever entered.

Other explorers are going into the very hearts of our largest springs. Most of us have absolutely no desire to be underwater and in a cave at the same time. Although some people seem to enjoy it, most of us would say it's risky. Mark Van Patten once received a jarring reminder of just how dangerous cave diving can be. I sat down with him in the spacious lobby of the Echo Bluff State Park lodge, a fire roaring nearby. Large, square-jawed and soft-spoken, Van Patten retired as a Stream Team Coordinator with the Missouri Department of Conservation. He has the distinction, in fact, of helping to form the state's first official Stream Team, the Roubidoux Fly Fishers.

Because he likes to fish Roubidoux Creek, Van Patten is very familiar with the large spring in Waynesville, called Roubidoux Spring, which provides much of the creek's flow. He visited Waynesville in the summer of 1991 to look at some repair work near the spring. The bluff above it had collapsed onto the road and crews had been working to remove the rubble. He was walking above the spring and looked down, into the blue rise pool, when he suddenly saw a "huge, black sea

*Dirk Bennett Cave Diving. Courtesy of Ozark Cave Diving Alliance.*

monster coming up." He chuckled as he told the story, but added, "it really did kind of scare me."[4]

The rising monster was actually a diver, a friend of co-divers Jerry and Angie Kennedy of St. Louis. The friend came up first. After a while, when he realized the other two had to be close to exhausting their air, he notified the police. A half dozen rescue divers were brought in from Ft. Leonard Wood and from other counties. Numerous dives turned up nothing. The next day, at 160 feet deep, the bodies were discovered, lying about twenty feet apart. He was 31, she was 25. Jerry had dived before but neither of them had cave certifications, and both had apparently ignored the warning signs posted in and near the spring.

Roubidoux Spring is a very popular diving spot. People come from as far away as Florida to dive there. But Florida springs are considerably warmer than Missouri springs. Over time, immersion in cold water, such as that in Missouri springs, can sap the energy and dull the mind. Experienced cave divers are aware of this danger and plan accordingly.

Dirk Bennett is one of those experienced divers. He's not afraid to scuba dive into springs. In fact, he says, it relaxes him. I met him at a coffee shop in Nixa, his home town, to talk about his chosen sport. He's short but wiry and strong and speaks in compact, measured sentences, maybe as meticulous about his words as he is about his cave-diving equipment. As president of the Ozark Cave Diving

84

*Divers in Blue Spring, Current River. Courtesy of Ozark Cave Diving Alliance.*

Alliance, Bennett helps organize diving projects in caves and springs all over the state.

I told him about Van Patten's experience at Roubidoux Spring. Bennett said he has dived into that spring numerous times, and "people will tell you there are dead people lined up in there, like walking through a cornfield."[5] Of course, it's nothing like that, but it's hard to blame people for their somewhat irrational fears. Many if not most people think cave diving is an inherently dangerous sport. Bennett, however, considers it to be safe as long as you know what you're doing.

There's a lot to know. There is a cave diving certificate for advanced "overhead diving" (i.e., you can't come up for air), with lots of technical training. You must have the right gear, which is highly sophisticated and expensive—except for the nylon line that is followed back to the entrance in the event of a "silt out." Newer DPVs (Dive Propulsion Vehicles) are powerful and can pull divers against strong currents, allowing them to go deeper and further. In order to get nitrogen out of their bodies, divers use different mixtures of gases. The precise mix depends on the length and depth of the dive.

Since the late 1990s more "habitats" have been used in cave diving. These are like upside-down boxes or rectangular diving bells, filled with air but submerged in a stationary position below the surface. Divers spend long hours in the habitat, decompressing. There are seats in there and divers will sit, legs drawn up out of the water, with their air tanks dangling on hoses below the box. They continue to breathe from their tanks. The habitat helps them warm up as much as anything. Hypothermia is a real danger for divers in the 58-degree F water of Missouri springs. That's one

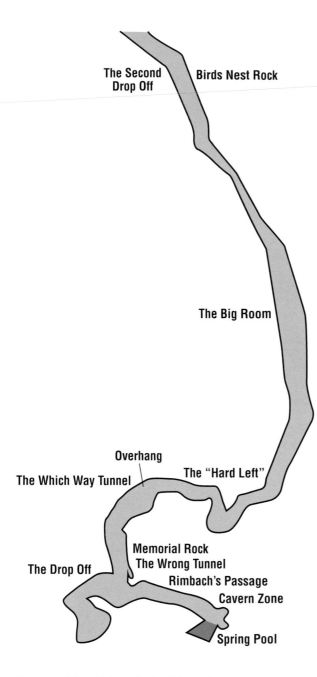

The Second Drop Off

Birds Nest Rock

The Big Room

Overhang

The Which Way Tunnel

The "Hard Left"

Memorial Rock
The Wrong Tunnel

The Drop Off

Rimbach's Passage

Cavern Zone

Spring Pool

*Portion of Roubidoux Spring/Cave Map.*
*Courtesy of Ozark Cave Diving Alliance.*

reason cave diving is so popular in Florida and Mexico, where the water is warmer and divers can stay under longer.

Dive safety is a primary consideration for Bennett and other professional cave divers. He strictly adheres to the "rule of thirds"—use no more than one-third of your breathing gases going in, another third coming out, leaving a third in case you need to get your buddy out. Using their sophisticated equipment and carefully scripted dive plans, Bennett and his cohorts in 2014 pushed Roubidoux Spring back 11,500 feet, two miles into the rock. They were underground for sixteen hours and up to 260 feet deep.

Divers also like Blue Spring on the Current River. This is one of Missouri's deepest springs, and arguably the bluest. The great depth at the orifice, about 275 feet, as well as the scattering of sunlight by tiny particles in the water (called the Tyndall Effect), creates an awe-inspiring blueness that almost takes one's breath away. In 2017, Bennett and his crew were immersed in Blue Spring for eighteen hours. They went back 6,800 feet, 3,000 feet of this previously unexplored or "new line," and were as deep as 315 feet.

Another Blue Spring frequented by divers, also called Davidson Spring, is no longer visible today—unless you're a diver. The outlet lies buried under twenty feet of water in Lake Wappapello. Described in Beckman and Hinchey's 1944 *The Large Springs of Missouri*, Blue Spring once flowed from a low bluff into the St. Francis River. Divers now call it Cannonball Spring, since a Civil War era cannonball, which may have been used as a boat anchor, was discovered there. Diving at Cannonball is a surreal experience. As divers head downward in the reservoir toward the spring outlet, they "go through murk and then all of a sudden it's crystal clear water."[6] Divers have gone down to about 380 feet in Cannonball Spring, as deep as any cave divers in Missouri have gone.

These divers aren't just seeing how deep or how far they can go. For the most part, their dives are not recreational, they're explorational. They gather subsurface hydrologic data. They shoot lasers to measure distances and make three-dimensional cave maps. They video cave features or the animals they encounter. Bennett distinctly remembers the first time he saw cavefish and how he marveled at their translucency. "I could see their hearts beating." Divers at other Missouri springs have also seen amazing things. At Sweet Blue Springs in Laclede County, divers saw an "underwater plume" of gravel spraying three to five feet above the cave floor. At Roaring River Spring, divers descended 224 feet into the spring before coming up into a gigantic, air-filled "dome room" that could only be reached via underwater passageways.[7]

I asked Bennett if he ever had any scary experiences diving in springs. The most "violent, dangerous" spot he's encountered, he said, is in Bennett Spring. The first constriction, the "keyhole," is about seventy feet down. Further down is an even tighter squeeze, where the upward current is so strong that it pushes gravel ahead of it as a "fluidized bed." It's like a "hurricane" in there, Bennett said. If you turn your head, it "rips your mask right off your face." "It's insane," he sighs, shaking his head. "You've got to be tough to pass that."

So, I asked, what is the reward? Bennett thought about this for a few seconds. "I guess it's when I lead a long dive and I think, literally, I've been where no person has ever been. That's the payday for me." Very few of us, of course, will ever have that kind of experience. I, for one, am perfectly content to relax in the sunshine by the spring, simply imagining what it would be like to be inside it, far underground. Often, I just sit by a spring and listen, sniffing the cool air. That's easy to do in my home town of Springfield, where several large springs form centerpieces of pleasant, grassy city parks. I sit and think about the appealing nature of springs, but also about their convoluted histories—histories that are interesting, but not always cheerful.

## CHAPTER 13: THE SPRINGS OF SPRINGFIELD

IT HAS OFTEN BEEN SAID that Springfield is named for its springs. Although that would make perfect sense, it's probably not true. There is no doubt, however, that springs profoundly influenced the development of the city. In fact, the first cabin in what would later become Springfield, built by John Polk Campbell, went up at the natural well, at a spot marked today in Founders Park. The natural well, really a skylight to the plumbing system of a spring, would later beget an urban legend widely circulated in Springfield—a theory, really, built upon two salient facts: a cave on the city's north side, conveying Doling Spring, opens northward, while a cave on the south side, containing Sequiota Spring, opens southward. A line drawn on a map between these two caves passes near the natural well, downtown.

Given this evidence, citizens could easily imagine that a subterranean lake lies under the middle of the city, tapped by the natural well downtown and providing flow to springs on both the north and south sides of town. This is almost certainly not the case, but the legend would be difficult to verify since quarrying and street railway construction in the 1880s obliterated any sign of the natural well. However, later excavations and construction projects downtown exposed underground openings that revived the story of the well and the legends surrounding it.

All of the large springs in Springfield are of historical interest. Both Sequiota Spring and Doling Spring were the sites of heavily visited "pleasure parks" long before they became city parks. At Sequiota, visitors could take a boat ride into the cave for twenty-five cents, carried on the waters of the spring. The Chadwick Line of the Frisco Railroad offered hourly rides to Sequiota Park on Saturday afternoons and Sundays. The spring supplied the Missouri Game and Fish Commission fish hatchery constructed in 1920, when the site became Missouri's smallest state park.[1]

At Doling Park, a large lake was formed by damming the spring below the cave. Visitors could dance by lantern-light at the lakeside, swim in the lake, or ride the "Chute-the-Chutes," a car that sped down an inclined track before plunging into the lake. At Woolen Mill Spring, earlier called Miller Spring, the first child to die in the new settlement was buried by a large oak tree at the spring. Later, the spring supplied water for the woolen mill and later still, the gigantic Grant Beach Park swimming pool.

Confusingly enough, there were two Jones Springs and two Fulbright Springs in Springfield. The "old" Jones Spring, earlier called Berry Spring, was located where the fountain at Ozarks Technical Community College is today. It was used during the Civil War for a federal convalescent hospital, served for a while as part of the city's public water supply, and later provided water for a bait shop. The other Jones Spring, on the east side of Springfield, was the site of Augustine Friend's "corn-cracker" grist mill built in about 1834. The mill used a pounding device powered by water in the flume, which was built using slave labor. The spring later supplied a distillery, but when the Civil War disrupted local grain farming its output was greatly reduced.

The "old" Fulbright Spring, on the west side of Springfield's downtown, was the site of many

*Boat Ride at Sequiota Spring. Courtesy of the History Museum for Springfield and Greene County.*

baptisms and served for a time as a backup for the public well on the Square. During the Civil War, this spring became the water supply for federal Fort Number Two, built on high ground overlooking the Jordan Creek valley. Soldiers accessed the spring from the fort by a covered walkway down the hill, providing them a degree of protection as they fetched water. The other Fulbright Spring, on Springfield's north side, became the city's first public water source in 1883. This had been the site of Fulbright's grist mill, built in 1832, which featured a huge overshot waterwheel. The spring also became a favorite picnic spot, for example hosting a giant BBQ in 1848 for heroes of the Mexican War.[2]

Several of Springfield's historic springs became casualties of urban development. Both the old Jones spring and old Fulbright Spring were covered up and obliterated by roadway construction; a city street for Jones Spring and a railroad for Fulbright Spring. Woolen Mill Spring, at Grant Beach Park, is now enclosed in a concrete box and discharges underground into the city stormwater system. Doling and Sequiota Springs still flow into city parks, but have seen their share of troubles from the urban development that surrounds them.

As Springfield grew, more and more springs were tapped for urban uses and many eventually

*Ritter Springs. Photo by Loring Bullard.*

became polluted and unusable. The first mention of water pollution in Springfield comes from the time of the Civil War and is blamed on the Yankees, who, being stationed on "foreign ground," carelessly trashed local springs and waterways. At Berry Spring, later called Jones Spring, Union soldiers washing their clothes in the spring branch reportedly polluted the natural well, downtown and a half-mile away, with suds, indicating a subsurface connection.

Springfield's first reported instance of chemical contamination of a spring occurred in the early 1870s, when citizens complained that colored dyes had tinted the spring branch downstream of the woolen mill. It only got worse from there. Edward Shepard wrote in 1915 that all of the old downtown springs were "more or less contaminated with sewage." At least one sinkhole was actually used for the "conveyance of sewage." In the 1960s, Sequiota Spring smelled so strongly of sewage that no one cared to venture near it.[3]

The pollution of Sequiota Spring illustrates the problem created when large numbers of septic tanks are placed in a spring's recharge area. By the 1950s, septic systems had proliferated on small lots above the spring, many of them on thin, rocky soils overlying cavernous limestone. The results were predictable. Tom Aley performed a dye trace in 1973, flushing dye down a urinal at Sequiota School and recovering it fifty days later at Sequiota Spring, 2,400 feet away.[4] When the city installed sewers in the area and eliminated septic tanks at houses, schools, and businesses, the spring began to clear up.

Jones Spring, on the eastern fringe of Springfield, has also had its share of problems. Conduits feeding the spring extend northward toward a sinkhole plain. When plans called for the new U.S. 65 Highway to cross this sinkhole plain, engineers didn't want water standing in a large sinkhole to flood the road. To prevent this, they placed a drain in the sinkhole prior to filling it. This drain, located between the lanes of the highway, allows runoff to flow directly into the conduit conveying

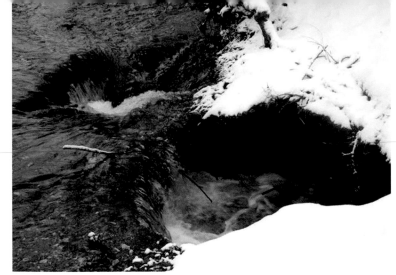
*Swallow Hole on Wilsons Creek. Photo by Brent Stock.*

water toward Jones Spring.[5] Unfortunately, this would also allow any spills on the highway to quickly contaminate the spring. Thankfully, that hasn't happened yet. However, chemical spills at industrial sites in the same sinkhole plain have tainted Jones Spring and killed fish in the spring branch.

On Springfield's south side, much of the subterranean flow goes to Rader Spring, Greene County's largest spring. Rader has the distinction of receiving much of the treated sewage from the city of Springfield. Wilsons Creek, both above and below the outfall of Springfield's Southwest Wastewater Treatment Plant, is a losing stream—water seeps out of the creek into conduits below. In the past, when Springfield's sewage was not properly cleaned, the foul effluent flowed down Wilsons Creek, with much of it disappearing into subsurface conduits. This created unhealthy and unsightly conditions in both Wilsons Creek and Rader Spring.

In the 1960s, low dissolved oxygen levels from the breakdown of partially treated sewage caused fish kills in Wilsons Creek and the James River, downstream. Even well into the 1970s, Wilsons Creek and Rader Spring were gray and turbid, and often had foul odors.[6] The city upgraded its facilities in the late 1970s and again in the 2000s, and now has state-of-the-art wastewater treatment. As a result, the quality of water in Wilsons Creek has improved markedly. It's a good thing, too, because the karst connections in Wilsons Creek sometimes take a dramatic turn.

This was aptly demonstrated in 2016 when a whirlpool developed in Wilsons Creek, a "swallow hole," which, at times, took all of the water from the creek and shunted it rapidly underground toward Rader Spring. The swallow hole became a local curiosity, warranting several newspaper articles and television stories. It grew ever larger, eating into the streambank, and within a few months another hole appeared a few hundred yards upstream, swallowing much of the creek's water. Fortunately, the water swirling and sinking into these holes in the stream bed was of much higher quality than it had been in the 1960s or 1970s.

These days, the city of Springfield and Greene County are more serious about protecting springs and groundwater. For the most part, pollution incidents like those described above are rare today. There is much more awareness of how vulnerable springs are to contamination, and there are better rules governing where and how potential sources of pollution are allowed, installed, or managed. Both the city and county no longer allow sinkholes to be filled, and both have setback and stormwater runoff requirements for land draining to sinkholes and springs. The city has purchased several acres of sinkhole-pocked land and removed chronically flooding homes, a move that not only prevents future property loss but should also improve groundwater quality.

Tim Smith, the engineer who once tried to remove the plug at Grand Gulf, recently retired as Deputy City Manager of Springfield. I asked him why Springfield and Greene County have become so proactive in protecting springs and groundwater. "People here were interested," he said. "We were a little more plugged in than some communities." He acknowledged the area's long history of spring pollution, but feels we've mostly risen above it. "To our credit," he said, "most of the problems are from the sins of the past. We didn't keep doing those things—both city and county recognized we needed to change."[7]

Because of forward-thinking leaders like Smith, there have been few incidents of spring pollution over the last two decades. But the sins of the past do still haunt us, occasionally. A case in point is Fulbright Spring—the old Fulbright Spring, near downtown Springfield, where the Fulbright family from Tennessee settled in 1830. At some point it was totally obliterated, probably by railroad construction in the 1870s. Amazingly, this original Fulbright Spring may have been accidentally uncovered during recent grading work at Jordan Valley Park in downtown Springfield.

Potentially, this is an exciting and historic find. But the newly uncovered spring has some obvious problems. It is contaminated with hydrocarbons, probably breakdown by-products of gasoline. When the spring was first uncovered, the smell was nearly overpowering, detectable in the air from many yards away. Sadly this, too, is part of the legacy of Springfield's urban springs— one that, hopefully, we now have the knowledge and means to prevent.

The other Fulbright Spring, just north of Springfield, became the city's sole source of drinking water when the waterworks were built there in 1883. At that time, springs were considered the purest and most healthful sources of drinking water available. Of course, we now know this isn't necessarily true. In spite of its vulnerability, however, Fulbright Spring remains to this day a major component of the city of Springfield's public water supply. It has provided drinking water to city residents for well over one hundred years. That, in itself, is a remarkable turn of events—and one to be celebrated.

## CHAPTER 14: POLLUTION FROM AFAR

ALL ACROSS MISSOURI, SPRINGS HAVE SUFFERED the same or similar fates as the ones in Springfield. We now know that springs are vulnerable to contamination no matter how remote they are. The karst channels weaving through bedrock, even reaching under surface watershed divides, knit together far-flung portions of recharge areas, producing subterranean arterial networks that can carry water and pollutants for many miles. This is difficult for the average person to visualize. As Tom Aley, owner of Ozark Underground Laboratory, puts it, we surface dwellers have a hard time "thinking three-dimensionally" about the land. But we're getting better at it. We learned this lesson the hard way at two of the largest springs in the Ozarks—Mammoth Spring and Maramec Spring.

Missouri could rightly lay claim to Mammoth Spring. While its outlet lies in Arkansas, just over our state's southern border, almost all of the water, of which Arkansas is the primary beneficiary, comes from Missouri. The spring gives rise to the Spring River, an immensely popular boating and fishing stream. The largest spring in Arkansas and third largest in the Ozarks (after Big and Greer), Mammoth Spring wells up into a tranquil, ten-acre pool before tumbling over rock and concrete dams and hurrying away down a scenic valley.

Mammoth Spring has long anchored a hydro-industrial center. The spring powered a flour mill on one bank, a cotton mill on the other, and produced electricity for the town of Mammoth Spring and other nearby communities. At one time, the area was remote and raucous. Spring City, just over the state line north of Mammoth Spring, boomed with booze joints when Missouri lagged behind Arkansas in enforcing Prohibition laws.

About forty years ago, disaster struck at Mammoth Spring when Missouri sent something south that Arkansas definitely did not want. Jim Vandike is one of the people who investigated the situation. I sat down with him at his home in Rolla over a bowl of deer chili as he described the incident. Wiry, with graying hair and beard, Vandike speaks softly but with the air of authority borne of many years working in the field. When I interviewed him, he had recently retired from many years of service in the Geology and Land Survey section of the Missouri Department of Natural Resources (DNR).

But in the late 1970s, Vandike was a graduate student studying karst hydrology in the North Fork basin in south-central Missouri. When his fellowship funds expired in 1978, he moved to Dora, a tiny town in Ozark County, where he took a teaching job. In May of that year, a sinkhole

*Mammoth Spring. Photo by Steve Spencer.*

suddenly opened in the bottom of the thirty-seven-acre wastewater lagoon serving the city of West Plains. Almost overnight, most of the lagoon's contents, about 30 to 40 million gallons of sewage, drained into the shallow groundwater system—a highly publicized wastewater disaster.[1]

Because Vandike had just produced new maps from his dye tracing work in the nearby North Fork Basin, he was called in to help. He assumed the lost sewage went to Mammoth Spring, since previous dye tracing had shown connections between it and sinkhole areas around West Plains. Sure enough, soon after the spill, bacterial levels jumped and dissolved oxygen sagged at Mammoth Spring.

As Vandike would later discover at Maramec Spring, even this horrifying incident could have been worse. The large conduits feeding Mammoth Spring allowed the sewage to speed through the ground like a shot into a jugular, seemingly polluting very few wells along the way. One well that did get hit served a restaurant, however, and at least one person suffered serious health effects from the spill. But the EPA felt that problems were much more widespread. After all, over 800 cases of "flu-like illness" had been reported in the area. The EPA recommended that an emergency water treatment plant be built at Mammoth Spring, but local officials argued that the plant could not be built in time to do much good.

The EPA sampled wells along the assumed underground flow path between West Plains and Mammoth Spring, finding that 30 to 40 percent of the wells contained coliform bacteria, indicator organisms that could mean sewage contamination. Missouri officials told EPA that these numbers were about "normal" for wells in the area, but EPA officials disagreed, publicly expressing shock at the large "zone of contamination." They stepped their sampling boundaries out even further, with roughly the same results. Their maps now showed a "huge area" affected by the spill.

It wasn't until EPA sampled wells tens of miles away from the spill area that the agency finally accepted what the DNR people had been trying to tell them—in a karst aquifer, and especially with older wells protected by shallow casings, a significant number of wells typically have high coliform counts—about 30 to 40 percent. After the spill, the sewage flushed through the groundwater system fairly rapidly. Within a few months, the bacterial levels at Mammoth Spring had returned to "normal" and dissolved oxygen levels had bounced back. The Spring River was once again pronounced safe for boating and bodily contact.

Just three years later, Vandike worked another major spring pollution incident—this time at Maramec Spring, which supplies water to a fish hatchery operated by the Missouri Department of Conservation. The fish, and the nearby Meramec River where many of the fish are stocked, are highly dependent on the amount and quality of water pouring from Maramec Spring (this is not a typo, the names of the stream and the spring are spelled differently—go figure). Large springs like Maramec and Mammoth have extremely large recharge areas, and are therefore vulnerable to problems from distant sources—exactly what happened at both springs.

In the fall of 1981, Vandike got a call from Mr. Gallagher, the manager at Maramec hatchery. Dissolved oxygen levels in the spring had dropped precipitously and the fish were getting sick. Aerators had already been brought in and fish were being moved to another hatchery. Trout were not the only animals affected, however. Crayfish and fish in the spring branch had died and cave crayfish had perished inside the cave, their ghostly white bodies flushed out into the daylight of the spring pool.

Vandike checked with a cohort, Jim Williams, who recalled that a pipeline had ruptured the week before near the small town of Lake Spring, about thirteen miles south of Maramec Spring. That was a long way away, but Vandike knew that the pipeline did, in fact, cross the large, previously delineated

*Cave Crayfish. Courtesy of the Missouri Department of Conservation.*

recharge area south of Maramec Spring. The old oil pipeline had been converted to carry liquid fertilizer, a mixture of ammonium nitrate and urea. The fertilizer also contained a fluorescent green dye, so that any leak that reached water would turn it a sickly, yellowish green.

That is precisely what happened. A landowner saw an unnaturally green pool of water in the creek on his farm and called the pipeline company, which responded quickly to find and repair the leak. The company estimated that about 1,200 gallons of product had been lost. Chemical testing showed that the tainted pool in the stream was "hot" with nitrate pollution. The company made plans to pump it onto adjacent fields for its intended use, as fertilizer, but as chance would have it, rains came before the company could act and the polluted water quickly flushed downstream.

Unfortunately, the stream below this point is "losing," meaning that most of its water normally leaks into the subsurface—into karst channels in the bedrock below the stream bed. In fact, the creek is totally dry except right after heavy rains—thus its name: "Dry Fork." The pollution moving downstream quickly seeped out of the stream and traveled at least 12.8 miles underground into the feeders of Maramec Spring.

Nitrate in fertilizer is readily taken up by plants, ideally by crops growing in soil. But in the groundwater system, it is food for bacteria. In the process of breaking down nitrates, these bacteria use up oxygen in the water. Below about five milligrams per liter of dissolved oxygen, trout become stressed, and below four they start going belly up. After the spill, the dissolved oxygen levels in Maramec Spring dipped to near zero.

As bad as it was, the mishap at least provided an opportunity to learn more about the spring's recharge area. Vandike also used the evidence to help determine the size of the spill and thus the liability of the pipeline company. He carefully watched the levels of dissolved oxygen, ammonia, and nitrates in the spring over time, finding that it took about seven weeks for the spring to fully recover. He also determined that closer to 24,000 gallons of fertilizer had leaked, twenty times the company's original estimate.

Not surprisingly, lots of homeowners near the spill or its assumed underground flow path were concerned about their wells. But of the 381 wells tested, not one was without doubt affected by the spill. Vandike thinks he knows why. Conduits to large springs like Maramec act like drains, which take in water, rather than like pipes under pressure that leak water out. A well that is very close to a conduit might be affected, but the pollution doesn't push out very far from the conduit. The conduit is a narrow flow path, and the chances of a well actually penetrating it are low.

Vandike thinks we were lucky that the pollutant was fertilizer instead of oil or gasoline. Fertilizer is very water soluble, so it flushed through the subterranean flow system rapidly. Hydrocarbons like oil or gasoline, on the other hand, float on top of water. When leaked into groundwater, they tend to remain on top of pools in the bedrock. Some product flushes out with each rain but a lot remains trapped in the ground as a continuing source of contamination. This long-term pollution can last for years.

The pipeline break at Maramec Spring was bad enough, but Vandike still worries about the "spill that hasn't happened yet." He remembers well the Shell Oil pipeline spill of Christmas Eve, 1988, the largest inland oil spill in U.S. history. Workers at a pipeline pumping station saw the pressure drop, but thought a gage was at fault. By the time the problem was discovered and the pipeline shut down, over 860,000 gallons of oil had spilled into the Gasconade River. A massive oil slick headed toward the Missouri River and the St. Louis drinking water intake. Though disastrous, the oily mess at least moved downstream fairly rapidly.

Further west, the same pipeline crosses the recharge area of Bennett Spring. What if the break had occurred there? You could've "kissed the trout fishing good-bye," Vandike sighed. The economic impacts would probably have been far greater than from the river spill, since the contamination would've lingered much longer in the groundwater. Vandike remembers a simple gasoline tank leak in the St. Louis area that polluted a small spring. It took years for the gasoline smell to clear from the water.[2]

Vandike is nothing if not pragmatic. "Pipelines are wonderful things," he said. "It's the safest and most efficient way to transmit fluids, especially high volumes of fluids. Can you imagine how many trucks it would take to carry that much oil? But how do you know when it's time to retire a pipeline? Does anyone look at that? Does anybody say they have to be x-rayed on a regular basis? We don't think of pipelines as contaminant sources until something happens."

Bill Duley is another former DNR employee who has seen his share of spring pollution problems. He was the Assistant State Geologist with the Missouri Geological Survey (a part of DNR), where his responsibilities included assessing the pollution potential of facilities such as landfills and wastewater lagoons. He also investigated pollution incidents. As we sat in a small office in Rolla, looking over some maps he had produced, I asked him about any memorable experiences with spring contamination.

One of the worst historical cases, he said, was at a small spring in Jefferson County. Health Department personnel reported that Kohl Spring had turned black and had a terrible odor. Dead insects had piled up around a hole in the ground nearby that was spewing gas. Even though this "blow hole" was located between Kohl Spring and a new landfill in the adjacent watershed, Duley's cohort blamed the water pollution on septic systems in the valley above the spring. The co-worker's reasoning was this: "It couldn't be the landfill" because it had a clay liner and "landfills with liners can't leak."[3]

The man believed he had a valid point, since the literature of the day indicated that a quarter inch of clay under a landfill should remove all contaminants. But practical experience had informed Duley that the weathered red clays over much of southern Missouri formed "little crumbly peds" that allow water and pollutants to seep right through. That is most likely what happened at Kohl Spring. A lesson was learned, and landfill liners are now constructed to be more protective of springs and groundwater. Duley told me that DNR has also attempted to prevent altogether the siting of landfills in karst settings.

After retirement, Duley returned to the Missouri Geological Survey to work on a special project to produce a new recharge area map for large springs in southern Missouri. There are lots of dye traces on the books, but Duley and his cohorts realized that some of these old traces should be replicated using newer, more sophisticated techniques. "It became a puzzle. You have to figure out where all the water goes. You don't know for sure which traces are valid. In some places, you have no information." Even new traces don't tell the whole story. "Traces show as straight lines on maps, but we know that's not true." The actual flow paths are no doubt circuitous.

*West Plains Lagoon Collapse. Photo Courtesy of Jim Vandike.*

The product of Duley's work is a map showing new dye traces and newly drawn recharge area boundaries (see pages 130-131). From this map, it can be seen that the recharge areas for some of the biggest springs in the state cover a large portion of southern Missouri. Big Spring, Greer Spring, Boze Mill Spring, and the Blue/Morgan Spring complex on the Eleven Point River get almost all of their water from the west. Mammoth Spring, Hodgson Spring, and Rainbow/North Fork Spring receive most of their water from the northwest. Hodgson and Rainbow Springs share a large recharge area. Some recharge areas send water in different directions to two or more separate springs. It's a complicated picture, but an important one.

This information is highly useful, because by knowing in advance which way pollutants would go, spill response should be much quicker and more effective. Knowing the recharge areas will also help in siting and designing potentially polluting facilities. We are lucky to have people like Bill Duley and Jim Vandike—people with an understanding of how karst works and know where to look for possible sources of pollution when springs become contaminated—and perhaps more importantly, to prevent such problems.

This is especially important if the spring is to be used as a source of drinking water. A few decades ago, there was a plan to bottle and sell the water of Missouri's second largest spring. This spring has a big recharge area, with several potential sources of pollution within it. But in this case, the quality of water at the spring was not the primary issue.

## CHAPTER 15: HEALTH IN A BOTTLE

YOU MAY REMEMBER that Greer Spring has a long and colorful history. Samuel Greer built a mill at the spring just before the Civil War, and a roller mill at the top of the hill in 1883. Luella Owens visited Greer Spring and wrote about it in the 1890s. Louis Houck bought the property containing the spring in 1904 and a year later, Edward Shepard of Springfield evaluated the spring's potential to produce electricity, but a hydroelectric dam was never built there.

Houck sold the property in 1919 to the Missouri Iron and Steel Corporation of St. Louis, which three years later sold it to the Dennig family. The Dennigs operated the 7,000-acre property as a kind of guest ranch for many years. When the Eleven Point River was designated Wild and Scenic in 1968, the parcel containing Greer Spring remained as the largest chunk of privately-owned, undeveloped land within the river corridor.

In anticipation of acquiring this land, the Forest Service, which administers the Wild and Scenic designation, had set aside $1.6 million to buy it, along with scenic easements on 2,000 adjoining acres. The Dennig family, however, refused to break up the parcel. Instead, in the early 1980s, the family seriously considered a proposal from the Anheuser-Busch Corporation of St. Louis, which wanted to bottle and sell about two million gallons per day of "pure Ozark spring water" from Greer Spring.[1]

The plan called for two pipelines to carry water from the spring to the top of the ridge where the bottling plant would be located. Anheuser-Busch promised to "preserve the integrity of the land and spring" by drilling a well into the cave conveying the smaller, upper spring, well back from the opening and out of sight of the public. Further, they promised to take and bottle only one percent of the spring's flow. Many Oregon County residents supported the plan, since it would create jobs and boost the tax base in an economically depressed region. Environmental groups, on the other hand, strongly opposed the plan, given the spring's ecological importance and proximity to a federally protected river.

St. Louis conservationist Leo Drey, Missouri's largest private landowner, became embroiled in the controversy. He later told historians about meetings between August Busch and the family patriarch, Louis Dennig, in which Busch suggested that he and Dennig each put a million dollars into the bottling plant. Dennig didn't have the money, he said, but he did give Busch an option on the land. Drey, viscerally opposed to the bottling plant, "put up quite a fuss" and "got some stuff in the St. Louis papers" about the project.[2] It was enough of a fuss, apparently, that Busch eventually dropped the plan.

Louis Dennig died in 1985 and three years later, Drey stepped in and bought the entire 7,000 acres from the family for $4.5 million. He intended to sell the land to the Forest Service at a reduced price, with the stipulation that all development be excluded, but the federal government had only authorized the purchase of a portion of the land. It would take an act of Congress to change that, a proposition strongly opposed by powerful legislators in Missouri who wanted to see that remarkable property made available for tourism, timber, and mining development. Doe Run also wanted to buy part of the land and trade it to the Forest Service for land near its mine in Viburnum, where it wanted to dump mine tailings.[3]

Drey was especially irked by the intentions of the mining company. If they came to him with an offer like that, he said, he would "throw them out of my office." Finally, after considerable coaxing, Missouri legislators agreed to sponsor a bill that would allow the Forest Service to make the purchase. Congress gave final approval on a voice vote in the Senate before sending the bill to President George H. W. Bush, who signed it. With this purchase authorization, Drey promptly resold the land to the federal government at a reduced rate ($500,000 less). Anheuser-Busch, perhaps to bolster its public image, kicked in $500,000 and made a generous donation to the River Network of Portland, Oregon. The 6,900 acres around Greer Spring became part of the Mark Twain National Forest, designated as a natural area and special preserve.

It would be easy to criticize Anheuser-Busch for even thinking about marring the stellar beauty of Greer Spring. But as always, there is context to consider. Prodigious quantities of clean groundwater surging directly from the rock almost beg to be used, somehow. Flowing freely through its marvelous canyon today, Greer Spring represents the notion that rare beauty and unspoiled grandeur can even, on occasion, trump utilitarian value. But in times past, water from many of Missouri's smaller and less charismatic springs did get bottled and sold. Bottled spring water was considered healthful—in many cases better for you than drinking from the public supply.

In the late nineteenth century, Missouri's citizens learned that disease-causing germs could be lurking, unseen, in their drinking water. This was before filtration and disinfection of public water supplies, many of which used surface sources. Fear of diseases in some sources, such as rivers or wells, led people to think that springs, and bottled spring waters, were safer. After all, this water had been filtered and purified as it percolated through the subterranean strata. Water from many of the state's springs—especially mineral springs—was bottled and sold from the 1880s through early 1900s, and Missourians drank prodigious quantities.

*Greer Spring Cave. Photo by Gayle Harper.*

Sales of bottled spring waters slumped rapidly after WWI, however. Francis Chapelle, in *Wellsprings: A Natural History of Bottled Spring Waters*, suggests that "bottled water went out of style in America on September 27, 1913."[4] That is the date the water treatment plant in Philadelphia first starting using chlorine to disinfect public drinking water. With this innovation, public water supplies became safer, eventually gaining back the public's trust.

Today, for entirely different reasons, bottled waters have made a big comeback. Per capita consumption of bottled water in the U.S. rose from 16.2 gallons in 1999 to 42.1 gallons in 2017. Spring water is a rising star within the industry, with the global bottled spring water market forecasted to grow over seven percent within the next decade. Growth is especially strong in "enhanced spring water," or water with ingredients conferring additional benefits, both for taste and for health.[5] With the rising concerns about plastics in the environment, it is today the bottle, more than what's in it, that concerns health advocates.

I wanted to know if any springs in Missouri were now being bottled, so I contacted Mark Jenkerson of the State Health Department. Unlike public drinking water supplies, which fall under the purview of the EPA (Safe Drinking Water Act) and Missouri Department of Natural Resources, bottled waters are regulated by the Food and Drug Administration (FDA) and the Missouri Department of Health. The FDA sets the standards for bottled water quality, and the Health Department inspects bottling plants for sanitation and good management practices.

After submitting a media inquiry and $42 to cover clerical costs, I received the list of Missouri water bottlers from the Health Department. It contained the names and addresses of twenty-three companies currently bottling water in the state, but didn't include information on whether springs were used as sources. Jenkerson estimated that less than twenty

*Bottled Spring Waters from a Springfield Supermarket. Photo by Loring Bullard.*

springs in the state were being bottled, but he couldn't tell me which bottlers were using them.[6] I decided the fastest way to find out was to search the websites of the water bottlers themselves.

To be clear, many bottled spring waters are sold in Missouri, but hardly any of them use Missouri springs. Perrier, one of sixty-four labels owned by the Nestle Corporation, is a famous example, hailing from the south of France. Hannibal, the story goes, drank from this effervescent spring while crossing the Alps in 218 B.C. This spring really is special. The water is an exotic mix of hot, volcanic mineral water and fresh water flowing through buried beds of glacial gravel. These qualities make the water fizzy with unique flavors and, apparently, eminently marketable.

For Perrier and other bottlers, protection of the source is a big selling point. Evian (which competitors like to point out is naïve spelled backwards) comes from a spring in the French Alps—from snowmelt that has flowed underground in a "protected aquifer" for "fifteen years." Poland Geyser Spring claims that its "alpine spring water" is the only bottled water in the U.S. captured directly at "authentic natural springs." The company uses seven springs, all in "protected areas" in California, New Hampshire, New York, South Carolina, Tennessee, and Oklahoma.[7]

Ozarka Bottled Spring Water, which may sound like it's from the Ozarks, is actually "A Source of Texas Pride." "Real Texans," the website croons, "know there's way more to their state than

*Glacial Erratics. Photo by Loring Bullard.*

dry and dusty deserts. There are vibrant, green landscapes where fresh tasting spring water flows from the ground." Ozarka uses three Texas springs— one just east of Dallas; one in the pine forests of East Texas; and the third near Lufkin in northeast Texas, "home to hundreds of dairy cows." Somehow, that last statement fails to inspire much confidence in the company's source protection program.

Closer to home, Mountain Valley Spring Water hails from the Ouachita Mountains of Arkansas, not far from Hot Springs. Said to have been the favorite of Calvin Coolidge, Eisenhower, Elvis, and Secretariat (the horse!), this spring bubbles up after a journey of "3,500 years through volcanic and sedimentary rocks, making it highly palatable and lightly effervescent." Presumably, the long length of time underground also renders the water remarkably clean and safe.

Of the twenty-three bottlers on the Missouri list, only four websites mentioned anything about offering spring waters. Puritan Springs of Earth City, near St. Louis, offers spring water for its St. Louis and central Illinois service areas, but provides no information on the spring or springs used. Waters of America LLC, with plants in Berkeley and Hazelwood, Missouri, similarly offers mineral or spring water, with no mention of sources. That leaves two bottlers: Missouri Goldfish Hatchery, Inc. of Stover, Missouri, and Premium Waters of Kansas City.

Missouri Goldfish is Randy Welpman's operation, which wholesales raw water from the spring near Stover that supplies his fish farm. The company website claims that the land where the spring emerges has "never been farmed." There has "never been any runoff from crop or animal production," it continues. Premium Waters once used this source but found a spring closer to its Kansas City bottling plant. Welpman, however, claims that his spring is better.[8]

Premium Waters, billing itself as a "consortium of bottling plants," describes three bottled spring waters on its website: Chippewa Springs, Nicolet, and Nature's Crystal, all in Wisconsin and protected by nearby national forests. Apparently, though, the company uses

*Basswood Springhouse. Photo by Loring Bullard.*

other springs that don't appear on its website. At a Kum & Go convenience store in Springfield, I bought a bottle of the store's own brand of spring water. On the label the source was given as "natural spring water," but there was also a telephone number for "water source information." I called it and Mrs. Atkinson of Premium Waters Consumer Affairs told me that one source for this water is "a Missouri spring." This turned out to be Basswood Spring, near Platte City, less than forty miles from the company's bottling plant in North Kansas City.

A few years ago, Kurt Hollman, a geologist with the Missouri Department of Natural Resources, was asked by Premium Waters to evaluate Basswood Spring for bottling purposes. Upon visiting the spring, Hollman noticed some odd, pinkish boulders sitting around. They seemed out of place for northern Missouri, and he recognized them as glacial erratics that had been transported to Missouri by glaciers from the far north, as far away as Minnesota. The boulders provide solid evidence of the area's interesting and eventful geologic history.[9]

The Basswood Spring environs were once a terminal moraine—a mound of rock, gravel, and sand deposited where a vast glacial sheet had stopped its forward progress. This deposit was later covered with soil and formed an aquifer, which cleaned and purified rainwater that seeped through it. In stark contrast to most groundwater in northern Missouri, Basswood Spring water is low in dissolved solids, and therefore good-tasting. Its unique geologic setting may also provide added promotional value.

With the increasing demand for spring water, bottling companies still search for candidate springs. Marvin Emerson at Crystal Lake Fish Farm was approached by the Nestle Company a few years ago. They took samples of his spring and measured its flow. Before they left, they assured him that if they used his spring, they would take only a fraction of the water. "Everything looked good," Emerson said, "but nothing has happened." He may never hear from the company again.[10]

Greer Spring, which Anheuser-Busch once planned to bottle and sell, would've been peddled, maybe very successfully, as a "pure Ozark spring water," protected by thousands of acres of surrounding National Forest. But with such a large recharge area, it's impossible to control for all factors that might affect purity. Municipal wastewater plants discharge treated sewage within the recharge areas of several of the state's largest springs, including Greer Spring. The wastewater is generally pretty clean, and it's cleaned up even more as it travels downstream, but it's still there.

These kinds of potential pollution sources within recharge areas may give bottlers second thoughts, as Jim Vandike discovered while talking to a man who was thinking of bottling the water of Hodgson Spring. The man seemed a bit taken aback when Vandike told him there were actually two municipal wastewater plants within Hodgson Spring's recharge area, not to mention a sinkhole dump about six miles from the spring. The man ended up dropping the plan.[11]

In spite of the evidence, many people remain unconvinced that anything bad could ever be lurking in such good-looking, good-tasting water. Bill Duley saw skepticism in the face of a woman who had paused by Boze Mill Spring to get a drink. "Isn't this the purest water in the world?" she asked him. "No, ma'am, it's not," he replied, and then explained that the city of Alton's wastewater lagoon discharged in the spring's recharge area, albeit many miles away. As Duley walked away, he overheard the woman saying to her friend, "I think he's just making that up."[12]

Seeing, to many, is believing, and when nothing can be seen in crystal clear, sparkling spring water, the possibility of pollution seems remote. Instead, what can be seen in a spring has often been taken as an indicator of its purity. When people saw fish or other animals living in a spring water supply, they weren't worried, historically—in fact, the existence of a thriving fauna has been taken as a positive sign. If the fish living in springs—or for that matter, shallow wells—were hale and hearty, then the water simply had to be good for people, too.

## CHAPTER 16: CANARY IN THE SPRING

PEOPLE BACK THEN PROBABLY DIDN'T EXPECT to see a fifty-five-year-old woman crawling on her belly into a low cave. But Ruth Hoppin was no wallflower. By the time she arrived in Missouri on sabbatical in 1888, she had taught school in Michigan and Massachusetts for almost forty years. Her teaching expertise was in biology, and her curiosity about the natural world led her to crawl into the little cave in Sarcoxie, Missouri. There, in a shallow pool not far from the entrance, she saw something she had never seen before—tiny, white, translucent fish.

A scientist at heart, Hoppin netted a few of the fish and observed them for several days in an aquarium before sending preserved specimens to Samuel Garmin, a zoologist at Harvard University. Garmin would declare the fish to be a new species, previously unknown to science.[1] It was similar to another cavefish, the Southern Cavefish, which had already been described from caves and springs in Kentucky. But this Missouri fish was distinctly different—more highly cave adapted, without even the vestiges of eyes.

The new species would be called the Ozark Cavefish and given the scientific name *Amblyopsis rosae* after another female biologist, Rosa Eigenmann, America's first female ichthyologist. In his descriptive paper, Garmin wrote that the Ozark Cavefish had to be related to the Southern Cavefish. But if Kentucky was their ancestral home, how did a cave-dwelling species get from there to Missouri? The huge Mississippi lowlands separated the two areas. Were there caves under the Mississippi River, or did the two species each evolve in place, separately?

Scientists still don't have all the answers to these kinds of questions, but they have directed a considerable amount of attention to the study of Ozark Cavefish. It is a threatened species, known to live in only about forty caves, springs, and shallow wells in southwest Missouri, northwest Arkansas, and northeast Oklahoma. It is indeed a rare and ghostly fish. Most people will never see one, because the little fish can only be seen in accessible caves and shallow wells connected to spring systems. These places represent tiny windows into the vast, pitch-black underworld where these creatures live. With such limited viewing areas, it is really hard to know how many cavefish are actually down there. As William Pflieger wrote in the *Fishes of Missouri*, "less is known about the distribution and abundance of cavefish than of any other fishes found in Missouri."[2]

Missouri has four species of cavefish, all dependent on groundwater. The Southern Cavefish is similar to the Ozark Cavefish, but is found more widely in caves and springs in south-central Missouri. A third species, the Spring Cavefish, has been found in only one location in Missouri—a spring-fed wetland at the foot of a bluff along the Mississippi River. Remarkably (for a cavefish), it has skin pigments and tiny, partially functional eyes. The fourth species is the most recently discovered, the white, blind grotto sculpin, found only in caves in Perry County.

Cavefish have well-developed external sense organs over their head and body, making them extremely sensitive to touch or vibrations. This helps them find their prey, and each other, in total darkness.

*Ozark Cavefish. Courtesy of the Missouri Department of Conservation.*

For their food, cavefish ultimately depend on nutrients brought in from the outside, since there is no photosynthesis in caves. Bat guano is one source of nutrients for the cave organisms fed upon by cavefish. Other nutrients wash in from the outside during rain storms. Cavefish feed mostly on "plankton," tiny organisms floating or swimming in the water, but will also eat larger animals such as isopods, amphipods and salamander larvae.

Cavefish are sensitive to pollutants such as fertilizers or pesticides that may seep underground. For this reason, the cavefish has become a symbol for groundwater health, like the canary in the coal mine is for air quality. If cavefish populations are doing fine, the theory goes, then there can't be serious water quality problems. This actually mirrors Missouri folklore. Cavefish were often called "well keepers" or "spring keepers," because their presence was taken as a sign that the water was clean enough for humans to drink.

In Missouri, the Conservation Department keeps close tabs on Ozark Cavefish populations, doing counts routinely at caves, springs, and shallow wells. About twenty-five locations in Missouri are known active sites, where cavefish have been observed in the past. At some sites, however, cavefish have not been seen for a long time. In 1984, William Pflieger, at the time a Fisheries Biologist for the Conservation Department, claimed that the Ozark Cavefish had "apparently disappeared from over forty percent of its historic locations."

With those depressing reports, new cavefish sightings are big news. There was jubilation in November 1996 when the Ozark Highlands Grotto, a caving club, saw Ozark Cavefish in Turnback Cave, the first sighting there since 1981. Jonathan Beard wrote that "the group rejoiced at the sighting of what may be America's rarest fish species. No more than two-hundred have been sighted since 1980."[3]

If found at all, Ozark Cavefish are almost always present in low numbers. There is probably not enough food in cave streams to support large populations. In 2016, during a survey of nine known cavefish sites in Missouri, eight fish were found in Sarcoxie Cave, the site of Ruth Hoppin's original 1888 collection. This was the most fish found at any one Missouri survey site that year.[4] The most ever seen anywhere, one hundred fifty, was in a cave in northwest Arkansas.

At the Missouri Department of Conservation's Research Center in Columbia, I met with Jacob Westhoff and Doug Novinger to discuss the plight of cavefish. They are very guarded about known cavefish locations, with good reason. Obviously, the tiny fish can be harmed by pollution or cave disturbance. But their numbers have also been reduced by collectors, even though it is illegal to collect them without a permit. Gates have been put up in the entrances of many caves to prevent poaching and disturbance of bat and cavefish populations.

"How far do cavefish travel?" I asked the Conservation Department folks, trying to imagine the little fish swimming in the eternal darkness below my feet. "We don't have a good feel for that," Westhoff replied. "When we visit a site, we see only a fraction of the population, especially at the well sites." Fish could be attracted to a well penetrating a cave or spring system, as this constitutes an "input feature," a place where bugs might fall in. Counting fish drawn to this source may skew population tallies and reveal little about the actual range of cavefish.[5]

Cave diver Don Rimbach witnessed the attraction of cavefish to the surface and its food sources when he entered a large sinkhole spring in the southeastern Ozarks. The spring pool is at the bottom of the steep-sided sinkhole, so is deeply shaded most of the time. This is one of the few places where cavefish have been seen in the daylight. During the dive, Rimbach didn't see any cavefish at depth. Rather, they were all hovering near the surface, in the top foot of water. To him, it looked like a "goldfish bowl at feeding time."[6]

Most cavefish sites are on private property. In a few instances, the Conservation Department, local governments, or conservation organizations have purchased sites, usually to protect a high-value cave containing cavefish. But purchasing is often not a feasible option, so resource professionals rely on cooperative partnerships with landowners—partnerships which include teaching landowners why it's important to restrict pesticide and fertilizer use in recharge areas. As Westhoff explains, "It's important to stay in touch with landowners; to let them know we're still interested."

Let's hope it's enough. Cavefish populations seem to be stable in some locations, and maybe the species will survive. But other spring-dependent animals are also in trouble, and the fixes are elusive. In Missouri, about forty species of animals are restricted in distribution to springs or subterranean waters. Some species are found in only one or a few

*Adult Hellbender. Photo Courtesy of Alicia Mathis.*

springs. When populations are small, conservation efforts can be more focused, but the risk of total extinction is also increased. One major pollution or disturbance event could take out an entire species.

One spring-dependent species in trouble is the Ozark hellbender, a large aquatic salamander that breathes mostly through its baggy skin. Hellbenders need cool, rapidly flowing, well-oxygenated water—in essence, spring-fed rivers. Unfortunately, their numbers have declined steeply over the past several decades, decreasing 75% since the 1970s. Causes for the decline are not totally known, but probably include several factors: a fungal disease, competition from non-native species, predation, over-collecting, and possibly, declines in water quality.

Most of the hellbenders collected today are adults; few juveniles are found, a distressing sign. One major reason is most likely predation of larvae by trout. Trout have been stocked in Missouri streams since the late 1800s, but stocking rates have tripled since 1960. Well over one million trout are now being released annually in the state's parks and management areas, and over half of the stocking sites are within the historic range of hellbenders.

Alicia Mathis at Missouri State University has spent years studying hellbender biology. In experiments performed by her and others, hellbender larvae in aquariums exposed to chemical cues from trout did not show a fright response. Clearly, the larvae did not recognize the non-native trout as a predator. Experimenters tried "training" the larvae by exposing them to trout chemical cues at the same time as secretions from stressed adult hellbenders. The trained larvae, when

*Tumbling Creek Cave Snail. Courtesy of the Missouri Department of Conservation.*

released into a river, might then be able to recognize trout as predators, so to fear and evade them, giving the little hellbenders a fighting chance to grow up.[7]

Large numbers of hellbenders are being raised in captivity with a view toward restocking them into suitable habitats. In 2016, the St. Louis Zoo and Missouri Conservation Department jointly released 1,310 zoo-raised hellbenders into Ozark streams. These populations will be closely monitored in order to determine the success of the restocking program. Locations where hellbenders are released are kept secret, because in the past, collectors have been a big part of the problem.

Many other spring and cave-dependent critters are in some degree of peril. These include the tiny Tumbling Creek cave snail, which as far as we know is found in only one cave stream in extreme southern Missouri; a tiny pink flatworm, found in only one spring at Rock Bridge State Park; and a rare species of isopod, a crustacean flattened top-to-bottom like an aquatic roly-poly bug, known only from a few springs in the St. Francois Mountains region.

Species like cavefish, hellbenders, and rare isopods and flatworms are all, to some extent, canaries in the spring. When something happens to them—if their numbers decline further or they disappear altogether—there is cause for worry. Poor quality groundwater is a threat to all aquatic species, and to species dependent on groundwater, including us. Aquatic ecosystems are fairly resilient, and can recover if given the opportunity, but past a certain tipping point, some of these species could disappear forever.

Sometimes, intervention is necessary—training a cadre of hellbender babies before sending them into the wild, for example, or preventing some curious aquarium buff from collecting the last cavefish or hellbender. The strange and wonderful creatures inhabiting our springs need, and deserve, our attention and respect. We have the knowledge and the power to give them a fighting chance. We simply have to find the will to do so. Pointing the way are human "Spring Keepers," people who care enough about springs and groundwater—and the life they hold—to take an active role in their preservation.

## CHAPTER 17: SPRING KEEPERS

WHAT DOES THE FUTURE HOLD for Missouri's springs? Will more of them be obliterated by development, diminished by groundwater pumping or corrupted by pollution? It's hard to say. But there is good reason for hope. We're taking better care of springs now than we did thirty or forty years ago. Some of the worst problems of the past are not likely to be repeated. One big difference today is that many dedicated people are working to ensure that springs and groundwater are adequately safeguarded.

On the front line are the spring owners themselves, who often place great value on their springs. One of these people is Bob Lovett, the owner of Danforth Springs in eastern Greene County. One sunny winter day I met him for a tour of his property. With his graying hair and tiny wire-rimmed spectacles, Lovett looks professorial as he recites the area's history. Near his property, he says, is the site of one of the earliest grist mills in the Ozarks, erected at a large spring by Jeremiah Pearson in the late 1820s—the same spring passed by John Polk Campbell on his way to the natural well.

Lovett found his land while looking to establish a pinetum—a place to grow pine trees and other gymnosperms, his favorite plants. One of the springs on the property, near an old homestead, was overflowing with trash. He bought the land anyway, partly because he felt an obligation to clean it up. I asked him why he thought someone would trash up a beautiful spring. "It was just very convenient for them, I guess," he said. "They pushed the trash and old appliances over the bank and the stuff went away—right into the spring."[1] Lovett understands the sensitivity of springs. He is very careful about applications of herbicides or other chemicals on his land.

On the west side of Springfield, Clear Creek Spring tumbles from a large cave. The property is owned by Russ and Susan Campbell. As we sat in their living room, sunlight pouring through immense picture windows, Russ told me about his attraction to springs. He speaks slowly, and with his slight drawl and dirty boots he might pass for a cowboy. He did, in fact, grow up in western Kansas, where there was little water—and what was there was muddy. He found himself irresistibly drawn to the clear waters of southern Missouri.[2]

The Campbells built their home on a bluff overlooking Clear Creek Spring, so were very upset when the spring suddenly developed a foul odor and grayish strands of slime covered the rocks. All of the fish in the spring branch and the upper part of the lake, just downstream, were killed. After some investigation by state and local officials, the cause was finally uncovered. Somewhat surprisingly, the contaminant was a food product—molasses. A waste hauler had been hired to remove the molasses from a damaged railroad car and transport it to a wastewater treatment plant. Instead, he dumped the goo into a sinkhole a few miles from Clear Creek Spring. The molasses leaked into the groundwater, where it was consumed by bacteria, using up oxygen in the process. Low dissolved oxygen killed the fish, and slimy bacteria feeding on the sugar covered the rocks. It took a long time for the mess to clean itself up.

*Loring Bullard and Bob Lovett. Photo by Steve Spencer.*

That was bad enough, but a few years later, the same waste hauler dumped chemical waste from airline toilets into a sinkhole in the same area, once again fouling Clear Creek Spring. The man spent one night in jail for the first incident and paid a fine, but was never prosecuted on the second, a fact for which Campbell is more than a little resentful. He remains vigilant, however, and will keep working to protect his spring. "There is a responsibility to owning a spring," he told me, nodding.

In the western part of Greene County, the Chiles family owns a remarkable piece of land containing a beautiful spring. The land also has a natural arch, towering bluffs, and a spring-fed lake. I talked to Dan and Margy Chiles at the kitchen table in their energy-efficient, fortress-like home. Dan inherited the land from his parents, who, many years ago, spotted a tiny land-for-sale notice in the newspaper offering a "unique opportunity." Developers had already built a dam below the spring and installed roads. Dick and Ellen Chiles could not resist this opportunity and bought the property.[3]

But one day Dick noticed a terrible odor in the spring. At about the same time, nearby neighbors noticed the same odor in their well water. Together, they went to the Missouri Department of Natural Resources (DNR) with the complaint. After some searching, the most likely source was identified—a dairy farm, over a mile away, where wastes from about 200 head of cattle had been allowed to run into a sinkhole. "He was polluting everyone using that aquifer," Dan said, disgustedly. "For twelve years, Dick met with DNR and local officials to try to get the pollution stopped. But that only happened when the dairy finally went out of business."

Chiles is a careful and meticulous caretaker of his spring. He readily invites a host of experts to his property for advice on management issues, and he especially relishes visits from biologists. When he had a nutrient problem that caused prolific growths of algae and water weeds in the lake, some experts advised him to use herbicides. But Chiles was reluctant. "This is people's drinking water." He's right. His spring water eventually reaches Stockton Lake, one of Springfield's drinking water sources. Instead of using herbicides in the lake, Dan and his brother, Mike, bought an aquatic weed harvester, a boat with a rake-like device on the front. Harvested weeds are removed from the lake and composted for use as fertilizer. Obviously, Dan and his family take their responsibilities as spring owners very seriously.

Some Spring Keepers are just very interested in springs and feel obligated to educate others. I visited with one of these people, Jo Schaper, at Young's Restaurant in St. Louis, over a basket of delicious fried chicken. When she was thirteen, Schaper went on a two-week family vacation to Alley Spring and promptly "fell in love with the place." Today, when she visits a spring with her husband, he soon turns away, ready to move on—but he knows to let her linger for a while. "It kind of feeds my soul," she sighed. "I don't know why, but it does."[4]

Schaper thinks people are naturally drawn to springs because they're "innately fascinated by running water." To her, springs represent the "visual impact of groundwater." This is important, she says, because a lot of people still depend on groundwater. They "aren't picking up the bucket any more, but if they're getting water from a well—it's the same water." She pauses to reflect. "Springs have been sacred sites for millennia. Mix that with the basic need for clean water and the science behind it, and that's powerful stuff."

Schaper feels strongly that education can make a positive impact on groundwater protection. Since 1988, she has maintained the "Missouri Springs Virtual Resurgence" website, found at *Jo Schaper's Missouri World*. "I'm proud to say I had this out before any government agencies posted springs information online for the public," she said. "When I was getting my mid-life geology degree, I called the USGS (United States Geological Survey) in Rolla for any spring data updates, and they referred me to my own website. That made my year."

On the eastern side of the Ozarks, not far from Poplar Bluff, Markham Spring is protected by Spring Keeper Brenda Shearrer. Rising in a U.S. Forest Service campground and recreation area, the spring forms an intensely blue pond before emptying into the nearby Black River. I once spent a night there in a drenching rain. My tent and gear were nearly floating before the night was over, but as the clouds parted the next morning, shafts of filtered light illuminated the azure pool at the spring. It was one of the most amazing and beautiful sights I had ever seen at any spring, anywhere.

*Loring Bullard and Todd Parnell at Tallman Spring. Photo by Steve Spencer.*

Shearrer gets this. She has been working for decades to keep Markham Spring open for public use, in spite of the Forest Service's intentions of shutting it down, or at least neglecting to care for it properly. She and her friends have hosted dozens of bluegrass festivals and other events to raise awareness of what a gem—what a crown jewel—this spring really is. And she and many others have volunteered countless hours to pitch in and make sure it does stay open—chasing after maintenance problems, cleaning up, policing the area. "I prayed," Shearrer said, when she heard of the Forest Service plans to close Markham Spring. "And then I formed a committee."[5] That's how it often works.

One "committee" in southwest Missouri, the Watershed Committee of the Ozarks, has been working for over thirty-five years to safeguard springs and other water resources. A program launched by the Watershed Committee in the 1990s called "Adopt-A-Spring" utilized trained volunteers to sample springs. The program was well-received and successful, providing lots of good baseline data on spring quality. But Adopt-A-Spring was grant funded, and—as often happens—when the money ran out, the program ended. Such is the life of not-for-profit organizations.

Today, the Watershed Committee operates the Watershed Center just north of Springfield, where many water protection strategies are showcased. Signs explain that this site is part of the recharge area for Fulbright Spring, the city's original source of drinking water. At Sander Spring, a sign discusses the concept of recharge areas and how dye tracing is used to delineate them. The Watershed Center is heavily used. In 2018, there were 173 separate field trips involving almost 6,000 individuals.[6] By educating visitors about the sensitive nature of karst and how to conserve and protect springs and other water resources, the Watershed Center hopes to cultivate new generations of Spring Keepers.

*Markham Spring. Photo by Steve Spencer.*

A kindred organization in southwest Missouri, the James River Basin Partnership, works to maintain and improve water quality in the James River and its tributaries and springs. In 2013, 2016 and 2019, the Partnership sponsored basin-wide water quality "snapshots." Volunteers sampled scores of river and stream sites, along with seventeen springs. Because all seventy sites were sampled on the same day, variations in quality that could be due to changes in flow or seasonal conditions were reduced. Over time, with a snapshot every three years, it will become easier to discern long-term trends that may be due to nonpoint pollution sources such as septic tanks and urban and agricultural runoff.

On a crisp fall day, I toured Jude Ranch in Webster County with one of the property owners, Todd Parnell. We paused to admire Tallman Spring, spilling over a cherty ledge in a pancake-layered limestone bluff; and then visited Ollie Lasley Spring, cascading down a steep slope through moss-covered rocks. Large, spring-fed ponds nearby were stocked with trout and bass and the old lodge, now demolished, once featured a spring flowing across the floor. Essentially, the ranch was built around its marvelous springs.

Parnell has been a university president and a banker, and he's also an avid outdoorsman and conservationist. Recently, he served on Missouri's Clean Water Commission. I asked him why he found springs so attractive. He waxed philosophically, poetically, about water rising "freshly cleaned and recharged" from the "soul of the earth, lifting all who linger near to a higher plane."[7] I guess it works that way for me, too. There is certainly more to springs than meets the eye.

If the Earth in fact has a soul, springs could well be its outer expression—conveying the sustenance of life, renewing our faith, refreshing our tired mortal bodies. If springs are indeed portals to a spiritual center, the confluence of living waters and everlasting life must be there. These concepts are deeply satisfying, lifting us far above the mundane world of water supplies, mills, or swimming pools. Without a doubt, springs lift me to a higher plane. So, like the other Spring Keepers, I will continue to linger near them. There are few places I'd rather be.

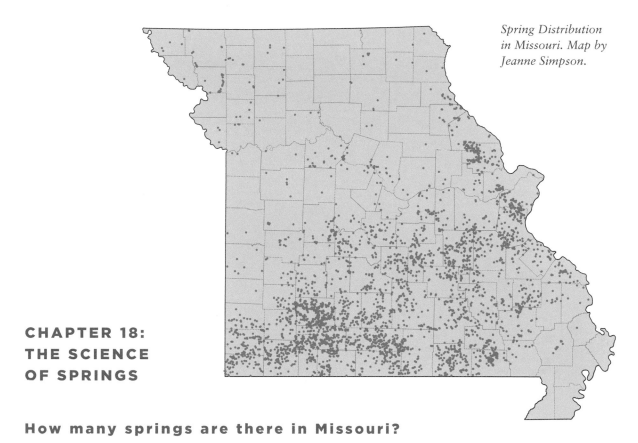

*Spring Distribution in Missouri. Map by Jeanne Simpson.*

## CHAPTER 18: THE SCIENCE OF SPRINGS

### How many springs are there in Missouri?

It is difficult to say—but there are a lot. Walter William's 1904 book, the *State of Missouri*, tells us that "by actual count," Webster County alone "has more than 2,400 living springs of clear water." It's hard to believe this was an actual count, but if it was, then there surely must be many thousands of springs in the whole state. Conversely, *Springs of Missouri*, the definitive work on Missouri springs published in 1974, noted "about 1,100" statewide.

The "official" count has risen dramatically since then. As of late 2017, The Missouri Department of Natural Resources database included 4,455 springs.[1] Most of these are perennial springs, those that flow continuously. On the other end of the spectrum, and generally not on the list, are intermittent or wet weather springs, which flow only after rainy periods. It is safe to say that while there are thousands of perennial springs in Missouri, there are tens of thousands that flow at least a few days per year.

## What are Missouri's biggest springs?

Big Spring is Missouri's biggest. It is truly a wonder to behold, its submerged throat erupting a full-fledged river. The surging liquid mass rises as a tumultuous, churning, crystalline dome. As a kid this sight mesmerized me, and still does. It is difficult not to stare, transfixed, at water that doesn't seem to behave normally—that is somehow lifted and animated by unnatural forces. And yet, it is a work of nature, and one of superlative hydrogeology, at that.

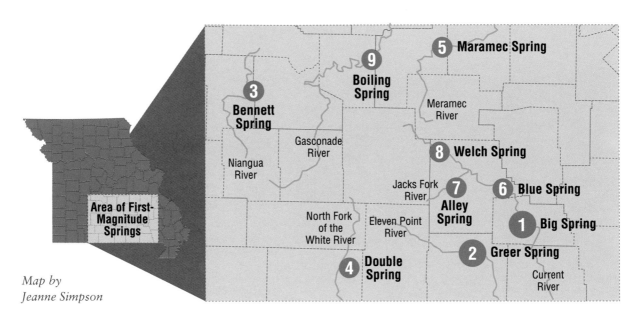

*Map by Jeanne Simpson*

## MISSOURI'S FIRST-MAGNITUDE SPRINGS

| Rank | Name and Watershed | Average Flow, cubic feet per second | Average Flow, million gallons/day |
|------|--------------------|-------------------------------------|-----------------------------------|
| 1 | Big Spring, Current River | 470 | 300 |
| 2 | Greer Spring, Eleven Point River | 360 | 233 |
| 3 | Bennett Spring, Niangua River | 185 | 120 |
| 4 | Double Spring, North Fork River | 155 | 100 |
| 5 | Maramec Spring, Meramec River | 149 | 96 |
| 6 | Blue Spring, Current River | 140 | 90 |
| 7 | Alley Spring, Jacks Fork River | 125 | 81 |
| 8 | Welch Spring, Current River | 116 | 75 |
| 9 | Boiling Spring, Gasconade River | 105 | 68 |

Big Spring is a first-magnitude spring, meaning that it is in a class with the largest springs—those with average flows of over 100 cubic feet per second, or 65 million gallons per day (mgd). (65 million gallons would fill almost 100 Olympic-sized swimming pools). Missouri has nine springs in this category. Big Spring averages about 300 mgd, over twice the amount of water used daily in St. Louis. After heavy rains, however, Big Spring can go up to 800 mgd or even higher.

Not surprisingly, the "bigness" of a spring is a debatable concept. Spring flows vary so greatly over time that unless they are consistently monitored, it is hard to establish an average flow, let alone a maximum. The famous Fountaine de Vaucluse in southeastern France, one of the world's largest carbonate rock springs, averages about 800 cubic feet per second (500 mgd), but with big snowmelts can produce almost seven times that much. Ice-melt rivers spilling from beneath huge glacial sheets in Greenland, technically considered "springs," can have tremendous flows but are almost impossible to measure, as are springs discharging below the surface of the sea. Crescent Beach Submarine Springs, a few miles off the Florida coast, is certainly one of the world's largest. It erupts from the sea bed sixty feet deep, and on a clear day the bulge it creates on the ocean surface can clearly be seen.[2]

Missouri's nine first-magnitude springs are found in seven river basins—the Current, Jacks Fork, Eleven Point, North Fork, Niangua, Meramec, and Gasconade, all in the Ozarks (see map). These big springs have formed within massive beds of limestone and dolomite in the Salem Plateau of south-central Missouri. Over long periods of time, the thick layers of rock making up the plateau have allowed huge spring systems to form. The networks of conduits feeding these springs, the plumbing systems, are three-dimensional, extending for hundreds of feet vertically and miles horizontally. The thinner layers of limestone on the Ozark fringes and the Springfield Plateau allow less room in the vertical dimension for spring plumbing systems to form, meaning springs there are generally smaller.

The amount of rock removed underground by the dissolving action of springs is truly prodigious. Big Spring, averaging 300 million gallons per day, in that same day dissolves away over 175 tons of rock. That's 64,000 tons of rock per year, the equivalent of creating a new underground passage each year ten by ten feet in cross section and over a mile long.[3] It could be an unsettling thought—springs continuously undermining the land, creating ever larger voids beneath our feet. But there is little need to worry. It's not as if a huge cavern is being created under any particular spot. Instead, the growth is spread out over many miles of conduits, each one slowly growing in size. And in most places, there's still a lot of solid rock between the conduits.

## Spring Names

Because Missouri has so many springs, over half of the springs in the state's database are "unnamed." Of course, many if not most of these springs once had local names, often now forgotten. Some of the most common names are rather unimaginative. For example, there are twenty-five Cave Springs, the most common name. Second is Blue Spring with eighteen, then seventeen Big Springs, twelve Twin Springs, and nine each of Roaring and Spout Springs. There are seven Elm and Rock Springs, six Boiling Springs, five Bubbling Springs, and four Rattlesnake, Dripping, and Stillhouse Springs.

*Big Spring. Photo by Gayle Harper.*

Spring names sometimes hint at interesting stories. A spring in Oregon County was named Sam Smith after a settler who was killed there by a panther, possibly because he wore a buckskin coat (Sam, not the panther). At Fishing Spring on the Meramec River, anglers dropped weighted lines into three portals in a rock shelf, pulling fish from the subterranean pool believed to lie under the bluff. Coffin Spring in Taney County took its name from the shape of the rock basin around it, and liquor was said to flow freely at Drunken Spring in Ripley County.[4]

## How do springs form?

Because humans both needed and revered springs, scientists weighed in early on what these manifestations actually were. In his 1664 treatise *Mundus Subterraneous*, the German Jesuit Athanasius Kircher offered an explanation that would stand for centuries. He hypothesized that seawater drained into holes in the bottom of the sea. High tides acted like bellows, pumping water to lofty elevations on the land where it emerged as springs. The theory rested on a verse found in Ecclesiastes Chapter 1: "All rivers run into the sea, and yet the sea is not full; unto the place from which the rivers come, thither they return again." Kircher thought that his theory offered an improvement over Aristotle's writings from centuries earlier. In this case, however, Aristotle had had it right.[5]

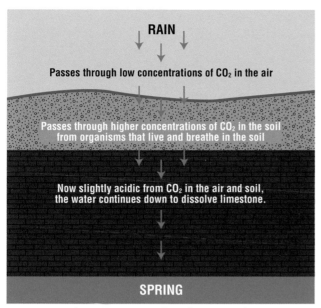

RAIN

Passes through low concentrations of $CO_2$ in the air

Passes through higher concentrations of $CO_2$ in the soil from organisms that live and breathe in the soil

Now slightly acidic from $CO_2$ in the air and soil, the water continues down to dissolve limestone.

SPRING

*Formation of Karst Topography. Illustration by Jeanne Simpson.*

It is little wonder that Aristotle speculated on the origin of springs, since Greece contains a lot of karst topography, the kind of landscape where springs form. In about 350 B.C., Aristotle theorized that the sun heated the oceans, evaporating water into the atmosphere. Clouds formed from this vapor, and from them, rains fell on the land, supplying rivers and springs with water. It is essentially the modern hydrologic cycle, taught in every middle school earth science class.

Missouri's early citizens were curious about springs, but they were hard-pressed to explain where all that water came from, or why it was so cold. Informed primarily by folklore and superstition, many of them embraced myths of far-off, exotic origins for springs, like water finding its way to Missouri from glacial lakes far to the north. These notions were firmly ingrained, held onto long after scientific inquiry generated better explanations.

Missouri's underlying geology is central to understanding the origin of karst topography, with its sinkholes, caves and springs. Over most of the state, bedrock is made up of flat-lying layers of sedimentary rocks. In the southern part of the state, these layers are composed mostly of carbonate rocks—rocks like limestone and dolomite, containing calcium, oxygen, and carbon—rocks largely made from the bodies and parts of animals living in the ancient oceans that once covered the region.[6]

Over the eons, organic matter settling to the bottom of these oceans formed thick layers of oozy mud; layers that were gradually compacted by the weight of many more layers settling on top of them. Eventually, the compressed material turned into solid rock—limestone and its close relative, dolomite, which contains magnesium in addition to calcium. These low-lying lands were eventually uplifted, seas drained away, and dry land, composed mostly of oceanic rocks, remained.

The rains came. Rainwater that couldn't find cracks in the rocky surface simply ran off to the nearest river. Where there were cracks in the rock, the water could soak downward. But if this downwardly percolating water couldn't dissolve the rock—and pure water could not—then karst couldn't form. In Missouri, many cracks have been opened into the carbonate rocks; and the water percolating downward isn't quite pure; it is slightly acidic.

These, then, are two keys to the formation of karst—pre-existing cracks and acidity. In the distant past, much of southern Missouri was uplifted from below by volcanic forces. The epicenter of this uplift, a rising dome of volcanic rock now called the St. Francois Mountains, ruptured and buckled the rigid layers of carbonate rock covering it, creating a network of fractures and faults—cracks—as well as producing gentle slopes away from the center of the uplift.

Acidity of the infiltrating water is explained by the fact that it has come into contact with carbon dioxide. This gas is found in the atmosphere, of course, but little of it dissolves into rainwater as it falls. In the soil, carbon dioxide is at a much higher pressure than in the air. This is because of all the organisms living in the soil—bacteria, fungi, worms, beetles, springtails, nematodes, and countless others—each breathing (technically, respiring), each adding a little bit of carbon dioxide.

Water percolating downward through the soil becomes slightly acidic as this pressurized carbon dioxide infuses into it, forming a weak carbonic acid solution—the same acid that is found in carbonated beverages. Now, the more acidic water can dissolve rock, enlarging fractures as it funnels through, always moving downslope. These enlarged openings, called conduits, gather even more water into themselves as they grow, and where this water finds an outlet to the surface, a spring is born.

The whole process is a bit of a chicken-and-egg thing, however. There must already be some outlet, or the water won't flow. If it doesn't flow, it won't dissolve much rock, because water in static contact with rock quickly becomes saturated—it can hold no more dissolved rock. So conceptually it's best to think of a spring system forming all at once—the input points, where the water sinks into the ground; the conduits or flow paths underground moving the water along; and the outlet, a spring.

Then things get really complicated, as they usually do in nature. For there is a wide variety of spring types, from little seeps along horizontal bluff partings to brawling boils in deep valleys. Karst doesn't form in a vacuum. While the spring's plumbing system is growing, other processes are going on at the same time. Rivers are down-cutting into their valleys, sometimes intersecting a spring conduit that was formerly underground; erosion is happening on the land surface, as well as underground. These ongoing processes, working in tandem, create a complex mix of spring settings and types that defy easy explanations for questions like, "How did that spring form?" or, "Why is that spring there?"

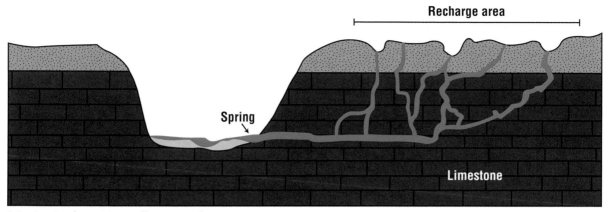

*A Spring Recharge Area. Illustration by Jeanne Simpson.*

## Where does all that water come from?

Where does the water supplying a spring come from? Usually, not all that far away. The surface area of land where this water is collected, mostly as falling rain, is called the spring's recharge area. You could think of the recharge area as the watershed for an underground river—one leading to the spring. The recharge area for a small spring is usually in close proximity to and just uphill from the spring. Larger springs have bigger recharge areas, of course, and some extend for many miles—but only for tens of miles at most, certainly not for hundreds of miles or further.

How can there be so much water coming out, day after day? It's hard to visualize, but there's a lot of water down there.[7] In well-developed karst, even if only one percent of the bedrock mass is composed of open spaces like fractures and conduits, millions of gallons of water will be stored or in transit within the recharge area at any given time. For us surface dwellers, who are used to seeing water flowing compactly in rivers or stored discretely in lakes and ponds, it is difficult to imagine just how much water exists underground.

The recharge area is probably a spring's most important feature, because what happens in that area is critical to the quality of water that emerges into the daylight. That's why we have to be so careful about installing septic tanks, pipelines, landfills, waste lagoons, or a host of other potentially polluting facilities within recharge areas. Pollution that is released onto the surface or into the ground can travel quickly underground to reach a spring.

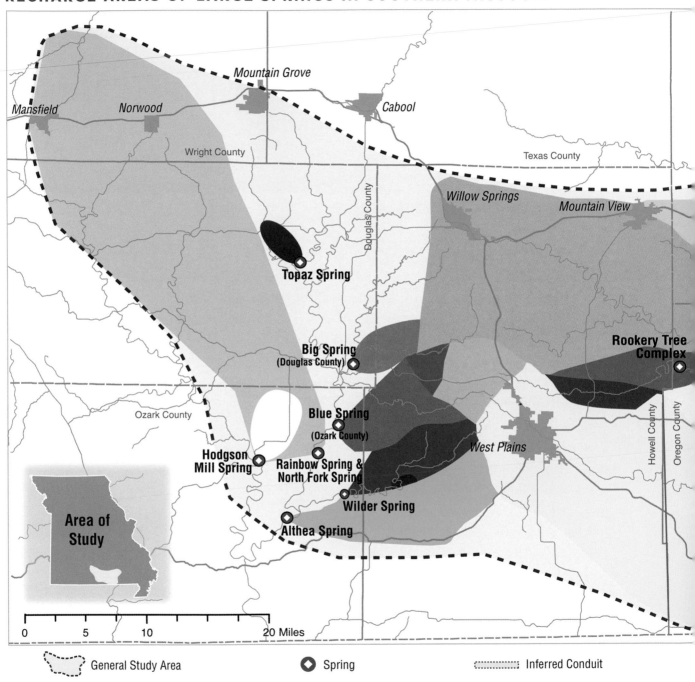

Mountain Grove

Mansfield    Norwood

Cabool

Wright County

Texas County

Willow Springs    Mountain View

Douglas County

Topaz Spring

Big Spring
(Douglas County)

Rookery Tree
Complex

Blue Spring
(Ozark County)

Ozark County

West Plains

Howell County

Oregon County

Hodgson
Mill Spring

Rainbow Spring &
North Fork Spring

Wilder Spring

Althea Spring

**Area of
Study**

0    5    10    20 Miles

⬦⬦⬦ General Study Area    ◈ Spring    ⠿⠿⠿ Inferred Conduit

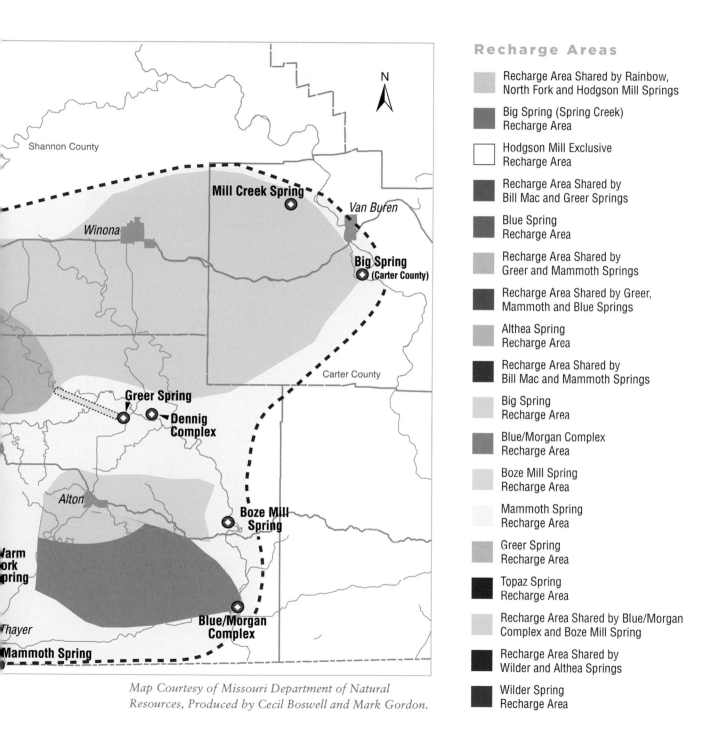

## Recharge Areas

- Recharge Area Shared by Rainbow, North Fork and Hodgson Mill Springs
- Big Spring (Spring Creek) Recharge Area
- Hodgson Mill Exclusive Recharge Area
- Recharge Area Shared by Bill Mac and Greer Springs
- Blue Spring Recharge Area
- Recharge Area Shared by Greer and Mammoth Springs
- Recharge Area Shared by Greer, Mammoth and Blue Springs
- Althea Spring Recharge Area
- Recharge Area Shared by Bill Mac and Mammoth Springs
- Big Spring Recharge Area
- Blue/Morgan Complex Recharge Area
- Boze Mill Spring Recharge Area
- Mammoth Spring Recharge Area
- Greer Spring Recharge Area
- Topaz Spring Recharge Area
- Recharge Area Shared by Blue/Morgan Complex and Boze Mill Spring
- Recharge Area Shared by Wilder and Althea Springs
- Wilder Spring Recharge Area

*Map Courtesy of Missouri Department of Natural Resources, Produced by Cecil Boswell and Mark Gordon.*

## Dye Tracing Missouri Springs

Dye tracing is used to determine where the water feeding into a spring comes from—delineating its recharge area. Some delineation work is fairly intuitive. For example, even a non-hydrologist could surmise that water disappearing at a losing stream might be the same water that reappears at a spring down-gradient and not that far away. Even a spring becoming muddy in the absence of rain can set up a kind of "trace."

*Dye Tracing. Photo by Jim Vandike.*

In the 1930s, for example, Alley Spring suddenly quit flowing, something the locals had never seen before. After a few hours, flow resumed, but the water was muddy for several days. It soon came to light that a sinkhole had collapsed about fifteen miles away shortly before the spring stopped flowing. A similar thing happened at Roaring River Spring in 1939, when a sinkhole pond near Washburn, about five miles from the spring, suddenly drained.[8] Drawing lines on a map between these sinkholes and the affected springs would delineate, or flesh out, a portion of their recharge areas.

Early delineation work sometimes involved some sort of "water tracing experiment." At Bartlett Mill Spring, the owner conducted a primitive trace by dumping chicken feathers into a sinkhole a few miles from the spring and later watching them emerge at the spring outlet. In a deep sinkhole in Carter County, curious tracers once placed a lighted candle on a plank and set it afloat on the stream crossing the sinkhole floor. They watched the light gradually disappear as it entered the sinkhole cave, heading, they theorized, toward Big Spring.

These days most groundwater traces involve the use of dyes. Scientists have largely settled on a few fluorescent dyes, chemicals which ordinarily wouldn't be found in the environment. This is important because the experimenter needs to be able to distinguish his or her introduced dye from natural substances found in the water. Fluorescent dyes can be used in very small amounts and detected by instruments in the laboratory, thus avoiding the embarrassment or consternation of turning springs bright red or green.

In preparation for the trace, field personnel consult geologic and topographic maps, making predictions about where the injected dye may emerge. These possible points of emergence, usually springs or wells, are then "bugged" by setting charcoal packets in them to absorb any dye that might come through. After sitting in the flow of the spring for a time, usually days or weeks, the packets are examined in the laboratory for the presence of the dye. The longest traces in Missouri have been about forty miles.

## Hydrologic "Budgets" in Spring Country

Dye traces can help researchers develop hydrologic "budgets" for karst river basins. Through dye tracing, for example, it has been found that in the Eleven Point River Basin, water in tributary streams leaks out, goes under a surface water divide, and comes out at Big Spring on the Current River. In other words, the Eleven Point watershed loses water through Big Spring into the Current River Basin. Using stream flow measurements and dye tracing information, hydrologists have determined that the Current not only "steals" water from the Eleven Point, but also from the adjacent Black and Meramec Basins.[9] The Black River loses flow to Blue Spring on the Current River and the Meramec provides water to Welch Spring on the upper Current. These losses from adjacent basins greatly bolster the flow of the Current River, supporting year-round canoeing.

## Why is spring water so cold?

So, the water supplying Missouri springs doesn't come from Canada or remote glaciers, as some folklore suggests. Then why is it so cold? The explanation is actually quite simple. Rock is an effective insulator, not readily changing temperature, so bedrock within a few hundred feet of the Earth's surface tends to remain at the average annual air temperature of the region where it is found. In Missouri, this is about 55 to 59 degrees F, north to south across the state.[10] Water traveling underground for many hours, days, or weeks eventually reaches the same temperature as the surrounding rock.

## Spring Oddities: Ebb-and-Flow Springs

Spring anatomies, their internal plumbing systems, can be very complex. Jerry Vineyard, co-author of *Springs of Missouri*, was intrigued by an unusual kind of spring called the ebb-and-flow spring. The flows of these springs tend to rise and fall in regular rhythms, irrespective of the time of year and largely independent of recent rainfall events. They are very rare. A roadside marker in Eminence states that of the twenty-three known ebb-and-flow springs in the U.S., five are found in Missouri, and three of these are in Shannon County.

This pulsing flow may have captured the attention of Native Americans as well as later settlers. The archaeologist Gerard Fowke claimed that the Indian name for Miller Spring on the Big Piney River, the state's largest ebb-and-flow spring, means "Breathing Spring." Blowing Spring, an ebb-and-flow spring in Howell County, was said to periodically make "queer noises" and blow out cold air, causing early settlers to think it was haunted.[11]

In a publication from 1923, Josiah Bridge speculated on what may cause the unusual behavior of ebb-and-flow springs. He suggested that their rhythmic action was most likely due to "internal siphons in the rock," an explanation that remains popular today (see diagram).[12] Jim Vandike has theorized that other causes may also be at work. Water building up pressure in gravel-clogged outlets, for example, may periodically break through the constriction, temporarily relieving the pressure.

*Top, View of Miller Spring at Low Stage. Below, View at High Stage. Photos Courtesy of Missouri Department of Natural Resources.*

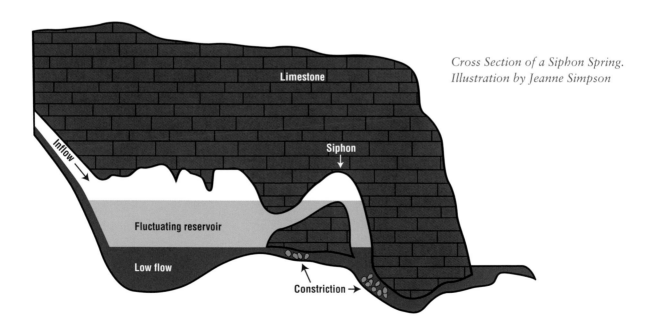

*Cross Section of a Siphon Spring. Illustration by Jeanne Simpson*

## Spring Life

*Bug Run. Photo by Bill Duley.*

Springs, and the beautiful rivers they sustain, are important to a variety of plant and animal species. Springs harbor life that is in many ways distinctive. The aquatic flora of springs is often their most eye-catching feature. Watercress, a tart-tasting member of the mustard family and a hallmark of Missouri springs, is commonly found in shallow, gravelly springs with swiftly flowing water. In larger springs, feathery fronds of water milfoil, ropy and luxuriant, waft in deeper currents. The spindly, narrow-leafed stems of water starwort can be found growing on muddy spring bottoms. Mosses and liverworts are common spring plants, as are red, green and blue-green algae.

Animals inhabiting springs must tolerate constant cold temperatures, so fewer kinds of them are found in springs than in warmer streams or lakes. But this lower diversity can be offset by large numbers of certain kinds of organisms, such as amphipods, snails, or flatworms. Springs are unique ecosystems, situated within the spectrum of habitat types between caves and streams, sharing attributes and life forms with both. Sometimes, animals adapted primarily to caves, such as blind cavefish or crayfish, are flushed or stray into the daylight of spring outlets. Conversely, animals will move from streams up into spring branches and cave mouths. Many kinds of aquatic organisms commonly inhabit both springs and creeks.[13]

The most visible animals in springs and spring branches are the fish. Fish commonly found in springs include sculpins, darters, and chubs. Wide-mouthed, sharply tapered sculpins, with their wing-like pectoral fins, burrow into the gravel of spring branches. Darters and minnows wearing exotic breeding colors in the spring, rivaling the fish of coral reefs, are seen by people bold enough to snorkel in cold springs. The creek chub is one of the most widely distributed minnows and is found in almost every small creek and spring branch in the Ozarks. Their nests are often visible on

*Niangua Darter. Photo Courtesy of the Missouri Department of Conservation.*

the stream bottom, consisting of small depressions flanked on the upstream sides by piles of gravel that the fish pushes into place or carries in its mouth.

Other spring-dependent animals include salamanders and frogs. Six species of salamanders are found in springs, including the white, blind grotto salamander. The most commonly seen frog is the pickerel frog, sometimes found in surprisingly large numbers in the cool basins of springs. Numerous smaller animals are also found, especially amphipods—crustaceans flattened from side to side, resembling miniature shrimp—and isopods—the aquatic version of the roly-poly bug. Crayfish are not well represented in springs compared to rivers, but several kinds occur in both. Two species of blind, white, cave-dwelling crayfish are occasionally found near spring outlets. Snails and flatworms are found in many springs and are often quite numerous.

Of special note to Missouri's fishermen, smallmouth bass thrive in clear, spring-fed streams. Native to North America, smallmouth prefer cool, clear, clean water. In fact, they have been found to gain weight more quickly in spring-fed streams than in other places. Pound for pound, they fight about as good as any fish out there. Most fishermen have their favorites, and everyone is entitled to their own opinion, but for my money, the smallmouth bass is Missouri's premier game fish.

*Rock Spring House. Photo by Steve Spencer.*

*The Spring House Painting by Andrew Wyeth. Photo by Loring Bullard.*

## Spring Houses

Springs serving as home water supplies needed protection from surface runoff and livestock, necessitating a sturdy enclosure around them—the iconic spring house. This building became the family refrigerator, keeping perishables a cool 58 degrees. Although warmer than today's refrigerators, the spring house worked reasonably well, preserving cured meats on hooks, crocks of milk or pails of butter placed in running water. At dairy farms, wooden or concrete troughs built into spring houses cooled rows of milk cans. Spring houses held the coolness inside, but also protected valuable food items from wandering marauders (usually, but not always, of the four-legged variety). Spring houses have been made of wood, rock, brick, or block.

## Indians and Springs

Native Americans were attracted to springs, just as we are. They used them for drinking water and bathing, of course, but also hunted animals drawn to springs and harvested plants growing in springs and spring branches. They also gathered the encrusted salt around saline springs and carried it back to their villages. Many of their habitation and camping sites were at or near springs. Jack Ray and Neal Lopinot, archaeologists at Missouri State University, told me that almost every large spring they have investigated has shown evidence of habitation—pottery sherds, projectile points, shell bowls, beads, scrapers, etc. Especially sought after were rock shelter sites near a perennial spring.

It is much more difficult, of course, to know what Native Americans thought about springs, since they left very few written records. Bruce McMillan, an anthropologist at the University of Missouri, suggests that springs were sacred places to many North American ethnic groups. This idea is backed up by the presence of burial sites such as those at Round Spring, which has, McMillan says, "five or six right on the rim." Springs were also believed to be portals to an underworld, inhabited by strange beings. "Water spirits were believed to dwell there, occupying the swirling depths of deep pools in springs or rivers." Further, some people believed that spring pools were inhabited by an "underwater monster," a creature often taking the form of a "panther, horned serpent, or other composite creature."[14] It isn't as far-fetched as it might seem. In fact, McMillan himself has unearthed bones of ancient, gigantic creatures at springs along the Pomme de Terre River—mastodons, the bones of which some Native Americans thought belonged to "Big Buffalo."

## Indian Legends

Not surprisingly, many of Missouri's springs have "Indian" legends associated with them. Some are almost surely fanciful, but others probably have at least a grain of truth. Here are some that I collected during my research on Missouri Springs.

**Monegaw Springs:** A widely repeated legend surrounds Monegaw Springs, now an end-of-the-road village in St. Clair County. The springs there, now covered by the waters of Truman Reservoir, were said to have been named for an Osage Indian Chief, Monegaw. The name, supposedly meaning "owner of much money," was applied after the chief recovered a cache of Spanish silver. According to the story, a dying Spaniard—the last of a group slain by Indians—disclosed the booty's location to Monegaw.

It would've been difficult, the legend goes, to find a "nobler Indian or a better specimen of manhood" than Monegaw. He was described as tall, strong and of great intellect. He must have also been prescient, because he foresaw the inexorable nature of the tide of white settlers. He told his braves to depart to the west, and in spite of his great wealth, lost all hope, starving

*Monegaw Springs Club. Photo Courtesy of the Missouri Historical Society, Columbia.*

*Blue Spring, "Mehaska." Photo by Loring Bullard.*

himself to death in a cave near the springs. The trouble is that no one seems to know for sure how much, if any, of this story is true, or whether Monegaw even existed.[15]

**Mill Spring, the "Spring of Death":** Another story revolves around a spring in Wayne County, the so-called "spring of death."[16] A band of Osage Indians, hunting in what would become southern Missouri, came across and attacked a group of Delaware Indians. The Osage killed all but one of the Delaware, the son of a chief, whom they took as a hostage. The young warrior was injured, feverish, and thirsty. Coming upon a large spring, the Osage devised a horrendous torture. They tied their dehydrated captive with his face excruciatingly close to the cool spring water, then cut off his scalp lock and left.

Searching Delaware finally tracked down their leader, but it was too late. This had been a cruel death, they realized, but they had been riding hard and were very thirsty. The mother of the chief's son, however, warned them against drinking, saying, "Would you drink of the water whose music tortured your brother?" Placing a curse upon the spring, she declared, "From this day, may all beast and man who drink of this spring sicken and die." Settlers later claimed that "disease lurked in it," and "cattle and wild animals will shun it."

**Mehaska:** Blue Spring, in Crawford County, was called "Mehaska," after an Indian maiden who accidentally tinted the spring when she dropped her bright blue cosmetics into it. The little branch flowing from this spring is now one of the few creeks in Missouri sustaining a population of "wild" rainbow trout. The Salvation Army's Camp Mehaska surrounds the rock-walled outlet of Blue Spring.

**Palmyra:** A French priest, in baptizing a chief's daughter, sprinkled her with water from Palmyra Spring. She was later captured by a warring tribe but they soon returned her, unharmed. The Indians believed that great magic in the spring had saved her life. Palmyra Spring issues from a stone-lined basin in a little park in downtown Palmyra.

# EPILOGUE

MISSOURI IS DOING A BETTER JOB of protecting its springs and groundwater, but there is room for improvement. We're still a long way from treating our springs and streams as "one interconnected and interdependent geologic organism," as Andy Ostmeyer suggests. From a practical standpoint, however, such concepts are difficult to translate into specific management programs. The public must support any new requirements or regulations that are deemed necessary, and costs will always be an issue. But as the state's population continues to increase, the need to properly care for our springs and groundwater will only become more urgent.

For ideas and potential guidance on ways to better protect springs, we can look to other karst regions. Florida has lots of big springs; in fact, more first- and second-magnitude springs than any other state. The largest of them are exquisite gems, heavily used for recreation—swimming, scuba diving, canoeing, and tubing. But many of Florida's springs are in trouble, their once gin-clear waters growing cloudy because of algae blooms and other problems.

In 2016, Florida's legislature passed the Florida Springs and Aquifer Protection Act. It identified thirty springs of historic or "special significance." Twenty-four of them have been found to contain excessive nitrogen, mainly in the form of nitrates, coming from sources such as urban stormwater, community wastewater, septic tanks, and fertilizer runoff from fields and yards. Nitrogen is a plant nutrient, and many of Florida's springs are becoming greenish and turbid from an overabundance of algae.[1]

The Act calls for the development of restoration plans, or Basin Management Action Plans, for affected springs, with estimates of the current nutrient loads, the prohibition of certain activities in recharge areas, prioritized lists of restoration projects, and phased milestones. The Act is fairly aggressive and for that reason will be difficult to put into play. Business interests will surely object to specific requirements. It is also largely reactive, of course, focusing primarily on restoration rather than prevention. But it's a start.

In Texas, the Edwards Aquifer underlies the western portion of the state. It is one of the most prolific karst artesian aquifers in the world. A unique ecosystem has evolved within the aquifer and its springs, including the rare Barton Springs salamander, the Texas blind salamander, and white, blind catfish, which have been pumped from wells almost 1,000 feet deep.

Barton Springs feeds a very popular, almost sacred swimming hole in the city of Austin, in use since the 1840s. In the 1920s the city constructed dams at both ends of the swimming hole,

*Reed Spring. Photo by Gayle Harper.*

creating a 900-foot long, semi-natural flow-through swimming pool. But in 1990, for the first time ever, the pool was closed to swimming due to contamination and problems related to nutrient-enrichment. Some of the problems have been dealt with, and the pool is open to the public today, but the threats persist.

Other Edwards Aquifer springs and creeks have suffered similar fates. Some of the best swimming holes now have "no swimming" signs posted. This, according to the Earth Justice website, constitutes an "inexcusable breach in stewardship." In 2008, a film about these problems called *Unforeseen* was produced by Robert Redford, who as a child learned to swim at Barton Springs. The film calls for strenuous actions to prevent further degradation of the state's springs.

The first legislation to protect the Edwards Aquifer and its springs dates from the great drought of the 1950s, but it dealt mostly with the over-pumping of wells. More recently, the Texas Commission on Environmental Quality developed the Edwards Aquifer Protection Program, requiring review and approval of plans for development projects in spring recharge zones. Sites are monitored for compliance with the rules.[2] But according to Earth Justice, "polluter lobbyists" have recently weakened legislative measures aimed at protecting water quality.

Missouri is certainly no more open to further regulations or restrictions than Florida or Texas. And yet, our state's magnificent, ecologically-critical springs must somehow be protected. Like most other states, we have a solid legal platform from which to build. We already have fairly good standards and rules in place for siting and design of potentially polluting facilities like landfills, wastewater plants, and pipelines. But like Florida and Texas, we are still very weak in managing or preventing polluted runoff from urban and agricultural areas.

Meanwhile, problems continue to plague some of Missouri's springs. In Springfield, local springs and groundwater have become contaminated with TCE, a widely used industrial solvent. Fantastic Caverns and the spring it contains have been found to contain worrisome levels of TCE from a circuit board manufacturing facility operating near the Springfield Airport from the 1960s until 2007. In the 1980s, wastes from this facility were placed into a shallow lagoon. Now, monitoring indicates that these wastes have traveled up to six miles in the karst groundwater system.[3]

Many springs in rural areas have elevated levels of nutrients, largely from animal wastes and septic tanks. High nutrient levels cause profuse growths of obnoxious, slimy algae. Even invasive species are encroaching into Missouri springs. Hydrilla, called the "Godzilla" of plant invasive species, is choking the life out of Wakulla Springs in Florida, and could eventually become a serious problem in Missouri springs as well. The pesky didymo, or "rock snot," is already invading Missouri's spring-fed streams.

Worldwide, clean water resources become scarcer every year. The great body of fresh water underlying Missouri is not just important—it is, in fact, a strategic resource. As supplies of fresh water dwindle elsewhere, businesses, other states, and even foreign interests will increasingly cast longing eyes on our powerfully flowing springs and clean aquifers. It is a good idea to safeguard these precious, finite resources. We should have learned by now that while a strong economy is important, losing our finest water resources to misguided economic pressures or unwise development would be no economy at all.

There are many benefits to living in the land of springs—but there are also added responsibilities. Vigilance and foresight are critical. We must learn to think three-dimensionally about the land, and find ways to safeguard our springs and groundwater for the long term. For this to happen, future Spring Keepers must somehow convince decision-makers that a strong economy and healthy environment really do go hand-in-hand.

I sincerely hope that my grandchildren, and their grandchildren, will be able to visit Missouri's amazing springs someday—and that they will find them just as beautiful, just as clean, just as refreshing as I have. Our wonderful springs are a legacy that should be handed down forever. It would be a very dark day indeed if the living waters ever ceased to flow—or became unrecognizable as the jewels they once were.

## NOTES FOR THE INTRODUCTION

1. The story of Campbell's journey to Missouri from Tennessee is told in the *History of Greene County, Missouri*. R. I. Holcombe, ed., Western Historical Company, 1883.

2. Alphonso Wetmore, *Gazetteer of the State of Missouri*, St. Louis: C. Keemle, 1837.

3. Edwin James, "James Account of S. H. Long's Expedition," in *Early Western Travels, 1748-1846*, Reuben Gold Thwaites, ed., Cleveland, 1905.

4. Milton Rafferty, *Rude Pursuits and Rugged Peaks: Schoolcraft's Ozark Journal 1818-1819*. University of Arkansas Press, 1996. Schoolcraft's approximate route and camping sites are located on modern maps in the book's Introduction.

5. "A Brief History of the Kansas City, Missouri Water Supply System," Appendix II, *A Geologic Cross Section of the Missouri River Valley at Kansas City, Missouri*, Missouri Division of Geology and Land Survey, Report of Investigations No. 72, Rolla, 1995.

6. *The Southwestern Journals of Zebulon Pike, 1806-1807*, University of New Mexico Press, 2007, accessed at https://books.google.com.

## NOTES FOR CHAPTER 1: ELIXIR OF THE GODS

1. Loring Bullard, *Consider the Source: A History of the Springfield, Missouri Public Water Supply*, Watershed Press, Springfield, 2005.

2. Interview with Tom and Sharon Vanderhoef, March 19, 2018.

3. Nelle Moffitt Allen, "Ye Olde Spout Spring," *Reynolds County Courier*, August 9, 1990.

4. Marcia Brown, "A Spring Water Connoisseur," *Ozark Mountaineer*, Vol. 44, No. 3, June/July 1996.

5. Interview with Creek Summers, November 18, 1979; *Bittersweet Papers*, RO669 Box 10, No. 323, "Springs," State Historical Society of Missouri.

## NOTES FOR CHAPTER 2: MR. KOCH'S SPRING

1. R. Bruce McMillan, "Objects of Curiosity: Albert Koch's 1840 St. Louis Museum," *The Living Museum*, Vol. 42 No. 2, 3, 1979.

2. R. Bruce McMillan, "The Discovery of Fossil Vertebrates on Missouri's Western Frontier," *Earth Sciences History*, Vol. 29 No. 1, 2010.

3. Thomas Jefferson, *Notes on the State of Virginia*, Penguin Classics, New York, 1999. Jefferson summarized information about springs in western Virginia, which at the time included a wide swath of the mid-section of North America. He described salt springs, medicinal springs, "syphon fountains," a natural well and a burning spring ("on presenting a lighted candle or torch within 18 inches of the hole, it flames up in a column of 18 inches in diameter, and four or five feet height, which sometimes burns out within 20 minutes").

4. Albert C. Koch, *Journal through a Part of the U.S. of North America in the Years 1844-1846*, Southern Illinois University Press, 1972; description of Koch's Missouri digs in an Introduction by Ernest A. Stadler.

5.  Albert C. Koch, *Description of the Missourian or Missouri Leviathan, together with Supposed Habits*, Louisville Ky., 1841.

6.  "The Missouri Leviathan," British Natural History Museum website, www.nyhm.ac.uk/discover-the-making-of-an-amercian-mastodon.html. Richard Owen, a superintendent for the museum, paid Koch $2,000 for the mount, plus $1,000 annually for life. Koch lived another 22 years, costing the museum about $24,000.

7.  Michael J. O'Brien and W. Raymond Wood, *The Prehistory of Missouri*, The University of Missouri Press, 1998.

8.  Interview with Bruce McMillan, March 6, 2018.

9.  *Prehistoric Man and His Environment: A Case Study in the Ozark Highland*, W. Raymond Wood and R. Bruce McMillan, eds., Academic Press, New York, 1976.

10. Modern African and Asian elephants apparently seek out natural mineral licks: "Elephants Eat Dirt to Supplement Sodium," www.scienceblog.com.

## NOTES FOR CHAPTER 3: BOONE'S LICK

1.  Fortescue Cuming, "Cuming's Tour to the Western Country 1807-1809" in *Early Western Travels 1748-1846*, Vol. IV, Reuben Gold Thwaites, ed., Cleveland 1904. This series is a treasure trove of stories about early North American expeditions and conditions.

2.  Interview with Neal Lopinot, January 11, 2018.

3.  Louis Houck, *A History of Missouri from the Earliest Explorations and Settlements until the Admission of the State into the Union*, Vol. 1, Chicago 1908.

4.  Most of the information about Nathan Boone's hunting and trapping adventures in Missouri comes from two sources: *My Father, Daniel Boone: The Draper Interviews with Nathan Boone*, University of Kentucky Press, 1999; and R. Douglas Hurt, *Nathan Boone and the American Frontier*, University of Missouri Press, 1998.

5.  Lewis Saum, *Research on Boone's Lick*, C2185, State Historical Society of Missouri Research Center, 1962.

6.  Garland C. Broadhead, *Report of the Geological Survey of the State of Missouri, including fieldwork of 1873-1874*, Missouri Geological Survey, 1874.

7.  Mark Kurlansky, *Salt: A World History*, Penguin Books, New York, 2002.

## NOTES FOR CHAPTER 4: HEALING SPRINGS

1.  John E. Sunder, *Bill Sublette: Mountain Man*, University of Oklahoma Press, 1959.

2.  Edwin James, "James Account of S. H. Long's Expedition," in *Early Western Travels, 1748-1846*, Vol. 14, Reuben Gold Thwaites, ed., Cleveland, 1905.

3.  Loring Bullard, *Healing Waters: Missouri's Historic Mineral Springs and Spas*, University of Missouri Press, 2004, in chapter "Springs of America."

4.  Diary of Samuel Custis, 1851, quoted in *Healing Waters* in chapter "Early Resorts."

5.  *Healing Waters*, in chapter "Early Resorts."

6.  Paul Schweitzer, *A Report on the Mineral Waters of Missouri*, Geological Survey of Missouri, Vol. III, Jefferson City, 1892.

## NOTES FOR CHAPTER 5: SPRINGS AT WORK

1. William Howard Norman, "History of Greer Mill," *Missouri Historical Review*, Vol. 66 No. 4, 1972; and Phyllis Rossiter, "Fabled Greer Spring: Tragedy and Triumph," *Ozark Mountaineer*, Vol. 41, No. 2, 3, April 1993.

2. "The Mill Acts," *Virginia Law Register*, Vol. 9 No. 4, August 1903, accessed at www.jstor.org/stable/1100475.

3. "The Old Schlicht Mill Still Intact, Goes Back to 1840," *Ozark Mountaineer*, Vol. 8 No. 8, September, 1960.

4. Fred Leach, "The Miller and His Customs in the Early Days," *Ozark Mountaineer*, Vol. 8 No. 4, May 1960.

5. Joe O'Neale Interview, *Bittersweet Papers*, R0669, Box 2 No. 73, "Topaz Mill," Historical Society of Missouri collections.

6. "Mills," Paul Wobis Collection, R008, Folders 2 and 3, Historical Society of Missouri collections.

7. "Zanoni Mill," *Bittersweet Papers*, R0669, Box 2 No. 058, Historical Society of Missouri collections.

8. Letter, Edward Shepard to Louis Houck, September 19, 1905, in *Edward Martin Shepard Papers*, Western Historical Manuscript Collection, University of Missouri, Columbia.

9. Luella Agnes Owens, *Cave Regions of the Ozarks and Black Hills*, Cincinnati, 1898.

## NOTES FOR CHAPTER 6: FOUNTS OF INDUSTRY

1. George C. Swallow, *the First and Second Annual Reports of the Geological Survey of Missouri*, Jefferson City, 1855.

2. Most of the information about the Maramec Ironworks comes from James D. Norris' *Frontier Iron: The Maramec Iron Works, 1826-1876*, State Historical Society of Wisconsin, 1964.

3. "Midco, Ghost Town of the Ozarks," in *Midco*, West Carter County Genealogy Society, undated.

4. Interview with Jim Vandike, December 11, 2017.

5. This and most of the following information on Midco came from the book *Midco* published by the West Carter County Genealogy Society.

6. Josiah Bridge, *Ebb and Flow Springs in the Ozarks*, University of Missouri Bulletin, Vol. 17 No. 1, School of Mines and Metallurgy, 1923.

7. Pig iron is unrefined or low-grade iron directly from the smelter. In the early days, the molten iron was poured into rows of closely spaced, roughly rectangular or oval troughs fashioned in sand. These rounded bars or dollops of iron apparently reminded someone of pigs.

## NOTES FOR CHAPTER 7: TROUT WATERS

1. Loring Bullard, "Natural Resource Protection 1904," in *Missouri Resources*, Vol. 22 No. 1, winter 2005.

2. Edward M. Shepard, *A Report on Greene County*, Geological Survey of Missouri, Vol. 12 Part 1, Jefferson City, 1898.

3. Ben Sechley, *A Century of Fish Conservation (1871-1971)*, U. S. Fish and Wildlife Service, accessed at http://training.fws.gov.

4. Kay Hively and Larry James, *At This Place: A History of the Neosho National Fish Hatchery*, Friends of the Neosho National Fish Hatchery, 2009.

5. Stephen E. Muich, *The History of Coldwater Hatcheries in Missouri*, Missouri Department of Conservation, 2013.

6. Interview with Skip Doak, December 12, 2018.

7. Interview with Chris Vitello, March 5, 2018.

8. Interview with Mark Van Patten, January 24, 2018.

## NOTES FOR CHAPTER 8: FISH FARMS

1. Interview with Larry Cleveland, September 9, 2018.

2. Interview with Randy Welpman, March 9, 2018.

3. Interview with Lisa Schleuter and Terry England, February 17, 2018.

4. Interview with Marvin Emerson, April 9, 2018.

5. Missouri Department of Natural Resources website, "Aquatic Animal Production Facilities," accessed at https//dnr.mo.gov/env/wpp/permits/issues/docs/G130000.pdf.

## NOTES FOR CHAPTER 9: SPRINGS AT PLAY

1. "The Clear Creek Swimming Pool," *Missouri News Magazine*, June, 1957.

2. John Bradbury, email January 5, 2019.

3. Loring Bullard, *Healing Waters: Missouri's Historic Mineral Springs and Spas*, University of Missouri Press, 2004. A visit to the ruins of the old swimming pool at McAllister Springs with my father, who swam there as a kid and who at the time lived in nearby Houstonia, helped to inspire the writing of this book.

4. Loring Bullard, *Jordan Creek: Story of an Urban Stream*, Watershed Committee of the Ozarks, undated. Information about St. Louis spring-fed swimming pools from an interview with Jo Schaper, December 22, 2018.

5. Kay Hively, "Mystery of Big Spring Inn," *Neosho Daily News*, November 4, 2014.

6. Interview with Robin Cotrell, November 29, 2018.

7. Jerry D. Vineyard and Gerald L. Feder, *Springs of Missouri*, Water Resources Report No. 29, Missouri Geological Survey and Water Resources, Rolla, 1974.

8. John Bradbury, "Nagogami Lodge," in *Old Settlers Gazette*, 2006.

9. "Traveler Savors Thoughts of an Earlier Pippin Place," *Springfield Daily News*, August 5, 1980.

10. "Pippin Place," Lynn Morrow Papers, R1000, folders 706, 707, 712, 714, State Historical Society of Missouri collections.

## NOTES FOR CHAPTER 10: SPRING PARKS

1. Missouri Life Inc. and Missouri Parks Association, *Missouri State Parks and Historic Sites: Exploring our Legacy*, Second Edition, Susan Flader, ed., Boonville 2016. This is an excellent reference on the rich history of Missouri's parks.

2. Interview with Bill Bryan, March 1, 2018.

3. Douglas Brinkley, *Rightful Heritage: Franklin D. Roosevelt and the Land of America*, Harper Collins Books, New York, 2016. I highly recommend this book for anyone interested in the conservation heritage of the country or the origins and development of the CCC. It is truly amazing the amount of land protected in parks, wildlife refuges, and conservation areas under the watch of FDR.

4. Andy Ostmeyer, "Will 20th Century Ways of Protecting Ozark Rivers be up to the 21st Century?" *Joplin Globe*, August 5, 2018. Ostmeyer has written a series of stories on the history of river protection in Missouri.

## NOTES FOR CHAPTER 11: SCENIC RIVERS, CROWN JEWELS

1. Interview with Oz Hawksley, January 28, 2008. I interviewed Oz in 2008 for a book I was working on at the time (and that was never completed). Oz was my major professor and leader of the "Outing Club" at Central Missouri State College (now University of Central Missouri) in Warrensburg. He was very interested in the cave faunas of Missouri, and rubbed shoulders with Jerry Vineyard and J. Harlan Bretz in some of Missouri's caves. Oz passed away in September 2017 in Medford, Oregon.

2. "Ozark National Scenic Riverways: Laws and Policies," National Park Service website, accessed at https://www.nps.gov/ozark/learn/management/lawsandpolicies/htm.

## NOTES FOR CHAPTER 12: EXPLORING MISSOURI SPRINGS

1. Luella Agnes Owens, *Cave Regions of the Ozark and Black Hills*, Cincinnati, 1898.

2. Interview with Tim Smith, December 12, 2017.

3. A detailed description of the Devil's Well and underground lake is given in *Springs of Missouri* by Jerry D. Vineyard and Gerald L. Feder, Missouri Geological Survey and Water Resources, Rolla, 1974.

4. Interview with Mark Van Patten, January 24, 2018.

5. Interview with Dirk Bennett, February 5, 2018.

6. Interview with Jo Schaper, December 16, 2018.

7. Jerry D. Vineyard and Gerald L. Feder, *Springs of Missouri*, Missouri Geological Survey and Water Resources, Rolla, 1974.

## NOTES FOR CHAPTER 13: THE SPRINGS OF SPRINGFIELD

1. Loring Bullard, *Jordan Creek: Story of an Urban Stream*, Watershed Committee of the Ozark, undated.

2. Loring Bullard, *Consider the Source: A History of the Springfield, Missouri Public Water Supply*, Watershed Press, Springfield, 2005.

3. Edward M. Shepard, *A Report on Greene County*, Geological Survey of Missouri, Vol. 12 Part 1, Jefferson City, 1898.

4. Tom Aley, "Groundwater Problems in Southwest Missouri and Northwest Arkansas," *Missouri Speleology*, Vol. 14 No. 2, 1974.

5. A diagram of the sinkhole and filling method is given in *Springs of Missouri* by Jerry D. Vineyard and Gerald L. Feder, Missouri Geological Survey and Water Resources, Rolla, 1974.

6. E. J. Harvey and John Skelton, *Hydrologic Study of a Waste Disposal Problem in a Karst Aquifer in Springfield, Missouri*, Professional Paper 600-C, United States Geological Survey, 1968.

7. Interview with Tim Smith, March 3, 2018.

## NOTES FOR CHAPTER 14: POLLUTION FROM AFAR

1. Interview with Jim Vandike, December 12, 2017.

2. Interview with Jim Vandike, December 12, 2017.

3. Interview with Bill Duley, February 16, 2018.

## NOTES FOR CHAPTER 15: HEALTH IN A BOTTLE

1. "Proposed Bottling Plant for Greer Spring," *Columbia Daily Tribune*, August 2, 1987.

2. "Reminiscences of Leo A. Drey, recorded on March 14, 1996," Oral History Program, State Historical Society of Missouri, 1996.

3. According to its website, the Doe Run Company operates "one of the largest lead mining districts in the world," as well as "one of the largest battery recycling plants in the world." Doe Run mines produced lead, copper, and zinc concentrates, https://doerun.com.

4. Francis H. Chapelle, *Wellsprings: A Natural History of Bottled Spring Waters*, Rutgers University Press, New Brunswick, NJ, 2005.

5. "Bottled Water: The Nation's Healthiest Beverage sees Accelerated Growth and Consumption," International Bottled Water Association website, https://www.bottledwater.org.

6. Interview with Mark Jenkerson, April 9, 2018.

7. Spring water bottlers websites, https://premiumwaters.com, https://www.polandspring.com, https://www.ozarkawater.com, and https://www.mountainvalleyspring.com.

8. Interview with Randy Welpman, March 9, 2018, and Welpman Springs website, https://welpmansprings.weebly.com/.

9. Interview with Kurt Hollman, February 12, 2017.

10. Interview with Marvin Emerson, April 9, 2018.

11. Interview with Jim Vandike, December 12, 2017.

12. Interview with Bill Duley, February 16, 2018.

## NOTES FOR CHAPTER 16: CANARY IN THE SPRING

1. Samuel Garmin, "Cave Animals from Southwestern Missouri," in *Bulletin of the Museum of Comparative Zoology at Harvard College*, Vol. 17 No. 6, 1889.

2. William L. Pflieger, *The Fishes of Missouri*, Missouri Department of Conservation, 1997. This is the definitive popular book on Missouri fish.

3. Jonathan Beard, "Sighted at Turnback Cave," *Ozark Underground*, Fall, 1996.

4. Jacob Westhoff and Doug Novinger, "FY 2016 Ozark Cavefish Monitoring," Missouri Department of Conservation, unpublished.

5. Interview with Jacob Westhoff and Doug Novinger, March 6, 2018.

6. Interview with Jo Schaper, December 23, 2018.

7. Alicia Mathis and Adam Crane, "Saving a Giant Salamander," *IRCF Reptiles and Amphibians*, Vol. 16 No. 1, 2009.

## NOTES FOR CHAPTER 17: SPRING KEEPERS

1. Interview with Bob Lovett, November 20, 2018.

2. Interview with Russ Campbell, June 1, 2018.

3. Interview with Dan and Margy Chiles, March 3, 2018.

4. Interview with Jo Schaper, December 23, 2018.

5. Interview with Brenda Shearrer, November 29, 2018.

6. 2018 Annual Report, Watershed Committee of the Ozarks.

7. Interview with Todd Parnell, October 16, 2018.

## NOTES FOR THE SCIENCE SECTION

1. The database of Missouri springs was provided by Kurt Hollman of the Division of Geology and Land Survey, Missouri Department of Natural Resources.

2. "Springs," Wondermondo website, https://www.wondermondo.com/springs/.

3. Calculations of the volume of rock removed daily by Big Spring came from *Springs of Missouri*. However, I believe there was an error in these calculations. It appears the number for the tons of rock removed in a year was overestimated by a factor of ten.

4. Most of the spring names come from the State Historical Society of Missouri manuscript collection, Ramsey Place Name File, found online at https://shsmo.org/ramsay.html. A description of Fishing Spring is found in the *History of Franklin, Jefferson, Washington, Crawford and Gasconade Counties*, Goodspeed Publishing Co., Chicago, 1888.

5.  Frank Dawson Adams, *The Birth and Development of the Geological Sciences*, Dover Books, New York, 1954.

6.  An excellent, non-technical book on Missouri geology is *Missouri Geology: Three Billion Years of Volcanoes, Seas, Sediments and Erosion*, by A. G. Unklesbay and Jerry D. Vineyard, University of Missouri Press, Columbia, 1992.

7.  Under the Salem Plateau of southern Missouri, where most of the large springs are found, lies about 233 *trillion* gallons of groundwater, about half the usable groundwater in the state. This and other groundwater facts are found in *Groundwater Resources of Missouri*, by Don E. Miller and James E. Vandike, Missouri State Water Plan Series, Vol. III, Division of Geology and Land Survey, Rolla, 1997.

8.  Jerry D. Vineyard and Gerald L. Feder, *Springs of Missouri*, Water Resources Report No. 29, Missouri Geological Survey and Water Resources, Rolla, 1974.

9.  Interview with Jim Vandike, December 12, 2017.

10. Interview with Bill Duley, February 16, 2018. I had always heard that Missouri springs are about 59 degrees. Duley informed me that after hundreds of measurements, his agency found that the statewide average was closer to 57 degrees F, with the range north to south in Missouri of 55 to 59 degrees.

11. Gerard Fowke, "Cave Explorations in Regions of Central Missouri," in *Bulletin No. 37, Bureau of American Ethnology*, Washington D. C., 1922.

12. Josiah Bridge, *Ebb and Flow Springs in the Ozarks*, University of Missouri Bulletin Volume 17, No. 1, School of Mines and Metallurgy, 1923.

13. *Springs of Missouri*, by Jerry D. Vineyard and Gerald L. Feder.

14. R. Bruce McMillan, "Underwater Spirits and Sacred Places: Artesian Springs in Southwestern Missouri," in *Plains Anthropologist*, 2018.

15. Loring Bullard, "Monegaw Springs," in *Healing Waters: Missouri's Historic Mineral Springs and Spas*.

16. Allen Hinchey, "The Spring of Death," in *Marion County Magazine*, March, 1904.

## NOTES FOR THE EPILOGUE

1.  "Protecting Florida's Springs," Florida Department of Environmental Protection, accessed at https://floridadep.gov/springs/protect-restore/content/protecting-foridas-springs.

2.  "Edwards Aquifer Protection Program," Texas Commission on Environmental Quality, accessed at https:///www.tceq.texas.gov/permitting/eapp/.

3.  "Fact Sheet on TCE Contamination," Missouri Department of Natural Resources, accessed at https://dnr.gov/hwy/sfund/doxs/litton-factsheet.pdf.

# INDEX

# INDEX

155

# INDEX

# INDEX

*Mill wheel at Turner Mill Spring,*
*Eleven Point River.*
*Photo by Gayle Harper.*